The Charismatic Code

Anthony B Wilson

Published by Anthony B Wilson, 2024.

THE CHARISMATIC CODE

First edition. September 30, 2024.

Copyright © 2024 Anthony B Wilson.

ISBN: 979-8227187390

Written by Anthony B Wilson.

Dedication

Dear Reader,

Thank you. Not just for turning these pages, but for opening your mind to the vast potential that lies within you. You've allowed me to share not just a perspective, but a blueprint for a life imbued with greater depth, connection, and understanding. In an age where distractions are constant and superficiality often reigns, you've chosen to seek something more. That choice alone sets you apart.

Think of this journey like a voyage through the cosmos. Every interaction, every relationship, is a star in the vast constellation of your life. And just as the universe is governed by laws that reveal the beauty and order in what might first appear chaotic, so too are there principles that can bring harmony to our human connections. You've been willing to explore these principles, to question, and to grow. That's the first step toward transformation.

The insights and techniques we've explored together aren't mere tricks or tactics. They are tools for elevating your life, for seeing the world not just as it is, but as it could be. Like a telescope revealing the hidden wonders of the night sky, this knowledge can help you perceive the extraordinary potential in everyday moments and the people around you.

By embracing these ideas, you are not only enriching your own existence but also the lives of those you touch. You become a catalyst for positive change, a beacon that others can look to. And in this interconnected journey, we find that personal growth isn't just about self-improvement; it's about creating a ripple effect that transforms the world around us.

So, thank you for your curiosity, your willingness to venture beyond the familiar, and your commitment to becoming the best version of yourself. The universe favors the bold, and you, my friend, are now equipped to explore its boundless possibilities.

With gratitude and admiration,

[Anthony B. Wilson]

THE CHARISMATIC CODE

BY ANTHONY B WILSON

"The Recipe of a Suave Man: Mastering Confidence, Charm, and Finesse"

Introduction: The Charismatic Code – Unlock the Secrets to Suave Success

Imagine walking into a room and immediately commanding attention—not by what you say, but by how you carry yourself. Picture holding conversations where your words effortlessly capture the imagination, and your presence leaves people wanting to know more about you. The truth is, every man has the potential to exude this level of charm and confidence. Yet, few truly understand how to cultivate the art of suave charisma. This book is here to change that.

In today's world, charm, finesse, and social intelligence are more valuable than ever. Whether you're navigating a high-powered business meeting, wooing a potential partner, or simply trying to leave a lasting impression, being suave isn't just about good looks or smooth talk. It's about mastering a combination of qualities that make you magnetic, influential, and unforgettable. The Charismatic Code is your guide to unlocking those qualities, transforming you into a man who walks into any situation with confidence, grace, and an undeniable presence.

But what exactly is "suave," and why is it so important? Traditionally, the term conjures up images of sleek, debonair men—James Bond types who are unflappable under pressure, smooth in their delivery, and effortlessly cool. In reality, suave men aren't born; they're made. The men who seem to have an innate ability to charm and navigate any social situation have spent years developing their craft, even if they don't realize it. Being suave is about more than just surface-level cool; it's about mastering your mind, emotions, and interactions. It's about showing up as the best version of yourself every day.

So why should you invest the time and energy into developing these traits? Because being suave is a superpower. It opens doors to new opportunities, strengthens relationships, and enhances your overall quality of life. Whether you're looking to improve your romantic life, excel in your career, or simply become the best version of yourself, the principles you're about to learn will help you achieve those goals.

<u>**Why Suave Men Win**</u>

In a competitive world, suave men rise above the rest. While intelligence, ambition, and hard work are essential, they're often not enough to set you apart. Suave men know that success in life is largely about how you make others feel. They understand that emotional intelligence and the ability to read people are just as important as technical skills.

This isn't just about being liked—it's about being respected, admired, and remembered. Suave men know how to lead without forcing others into submission. They can inspire without giving a motivational speech. They navigate difficult situations with poise, whether it's negotiating a business deal or diffusing a tense argument. In short, suave men have a unique advantage because they make others feel at ease while remaining in control.

But how do you go from being an average guy to becoming that suave, magnetic figure? It starts with understanding the key components of charm, confidence, and social finesse. This book will break down those components into simple, actionable steps that anyone can follow.

<u>The Recipe for Charm and Finesse</u>

Many men assume that charm is an innate quality—something you either have or you don't. The truth is, anyone can learn how to be charming, but it requires self-awareness and practice. Charm is not just about saying the right thing; it's about how you present yourself, how you engage with others, and how you make them feel.

The foundation of charm lies in emotional intelligence, the ability to understand and manage your own emotions while also recognizing and influencing the emotions of others. Suave men are masters of emotional intelligence—they know how to read the room, how to tailor their approach to different personalities, and how to navigate social dynamics with ease.

Another critical aspect of being suave is confidence. Confidence isn't about being loud or arrogant; it's about being comfortable in your own skin. It's about knowing who you are, embracing your strengths, and accepting your weaknesses without feeling the need to apologize for them. The confidence of a suave man radiates from within, and it draws people in naturally. When you're confident, others feel confident in your presence.

Of course, confidence and charm alone won't take you all the way. Finesse is the glue that holds it all together. It's the subtle art of knowing when to speak and when to listen, how to assert yourself without coming off as aggressive, and how to maintain composure even in the most high-pressure situations. Finesse is what makes suave men stand out in a crowd—it's the quiet assurance that everything is under control, even when it isn't.

The Transformation

As you dive into this book, you'll begin to see a transformation in how you approach social situations, relationships, and even your own mindset. Each chapter is designed to build upon the last, helping you develop the habits, mindset, and skills of a truly suave man. You'll learn how to project confidence without arrogance, how to engage others with ease, and how to leave a lasting impression in any interaction.

But this transformation won't happen overnight. Like any skill, mastering the art of being suave takes time and practice. You'll need to push yourself outside of your comfort zone, challenge your current habits, and embrace a new way of thinking. However, the rewards are worth it. The principles outlined in this book will not only help you become more charming and confident, but they'll also improve your emotional intelligence, enhance your relationships, and open doors to new opportunities.

A Final Word Before We Begin

Being a suave man is about more than just surface-level charm. It's about mastering the deeper aspects of who you are and how you interact with the world. It's about cultivating a presence that commands respect, admiration, and trust. By the time you finish this book, you'll have the tools to transform into a man who is not only suave but also genuinely magnetic—someone who lights up every room they enter and leaves a lasting impact wherever they go. Welcome to **The Charismatic Code**. *Your journey to suave success starts now.*

Table of content

Table of Contents

Chapter 1: The Foundation of Charm – Building Unshakable Confidence

<u>Section 1: Understanding Confidence</u>

- *What Confidence Really Is*

o The difference between true confidence and arrogance.

o Internal vs. external validation: Shifting the focus.

o Confidence as the bedrock of charm.

- *Why People Are Attracted to Confidence*

o Psychological effects of confidence on social dynamics.

o How confident energy influences perception.

o The role of body language in displaying confidence.

- *Overcoming Self-Doubt*

o Techniques for quieting the inner critic.

o Reframing past failures as growth opportunities.

o Embracing vulnerability as a strength.

<u>Section 2: Daily Confidence-Building Habits</u>

- *Morning Rituals for Success*

o How affirmations set the tone for your day.

o Building a powerful morning routine to start strong.

o Visualization techniques for future success.

- *Body and Mind Connection*

o Physical fitness and how it impacts mental clarity and confidence.

o Breathing exercises for calm under pressure.

o Meditation and mindfulness for emotional control.

● *The Power of Preparation*

o Why preparation builds confidence in social settings.

o Mental rehearsals for difficult conversations or meetings.

o Developing expertise in areas that boost your confidence.

Section 3: Projecting Confidence to Others

● *Mastering Body Language*

o Posture: Standing tall and looking in control.

o Eye contact: How to use it to build rapport and authority.

o The confident handshake: Making the right impression.

● *Conversational Confidence*

o Speaking clearly and assertively.

o Knowing when to listen vs. when to speak.

o Dealing with criticism and staying poised.

● *Owning Your Presence*

o Walking into a room with purpose.

o How to engage a crowd with energy.

o Owning mistakes confidently: Turning failure into a tool.

Chapter 2: Mastering the First Impression – How to Make Every Interaction Count

Section 1: The Psychology of First Impressions

- *Why First Impressions Matter*
  - The science behind how we form judgments within seconds.
  - How these judgments impact long-term relationships.
  - Overcoming negative first impressions if they go wrong.

- *The Halo Effect*
  - What it is and how to use it to your advantage.
  - Why appearing well-rounded elevates your charm.
  - Examples of people using the Halo Effect effectively.

- *Creating a Memorable Introduction*
  - The art of the perfect introduction.
  - Shaping your personal brand with how you introduce yourself.
  - Using humor and curiosity to stand out.

Section 2: Dressing for Success

- *Style as a Reflection of Inner Confidence*
  - How your clothes communicate personality and confidence.
  - Building a wardrobe that matches your lifestyle and ambitions.
  - Why fit, color, and attention to detail matter.

- *The Suave Man's Guide to Grooming*
  - Daily grooming habits that make a difference.
  - Subtle details: Scent, hair, and accessories.

○ Techniques to truly listen and understand, not just respond.

○ How listening boosts your likability and charm.

○ Reading between the lines: Picking up on what's unsaid.

● *Asking the Right Questions*

○ How to ask open-ended questions that spark deeper conversation.

○ Using curiosity to make others feel valued.

○ Balancing conversation: When to speak and when to listen.

● *The Power of Storytelling*

○ Why stories are a powerful tool for connection.

○ How to share personal anecdotes without oversharing.

○ Building emotional resonance through compelling narratives.

Section 2: Navigating Difficult Conversations

● *Staying Cool Under Pressure*

○ Techniques to stay calm in heated discussions.

○ Turning confrontation into productive dialogue.

○ How to respectfully disagree while maintaining charm.

● *Dealing with Criticism Gracefully*

○ How to accept feedback without getting defensive.

○ Using criticism as a tool for growth and improvement.

○ Responding to insults with class and composure.

● *Keeping Boundaries While Staying Suave*

○ How to assert yourself without being aggressive.

○ Politely saying "no" while protecting your time and energy.

○ Maintaining boundaries in professional and social settings.

Section 3: Becoming a Social Chameleon

- *Adapting to Different Social Environments*

○ How to be at ease in any situation, from boardrooms to bars.

○ Adjusting your style of conversation to fit the setting.

○ Reading the energy of the room and blending in seamlessly.

- *Building Rapport with Anyone*

○ Finding common ground with people from all walks of life.

○ The power of empathy in building instant rapport.

○ How to connect with different personality types effortlessly.

- *Leaving a Lasting Impression*

○ How to wrap up conversations in a memorable way.

○ Creating an air of intrigue and leaving people wanting more.

○ Maintaining connections after the initial meeting.

Chapter 4: The Art of Persuasion – Influencing People Without Being Pushy

Section 1: The Psychology of Persuasion

- *The Principles of Influence*

○ How reciprocity, scarcity, and authority shape behavior.

○ Building trust as the foundation for influence.

○ Understanding emotional triggers to persuade effectively.

● *Subtle Persuasion Techniques*

○ How to suggest rather than demand.

○ Using body language and tone of voice to persuade.

○ The power of gentle nudging vs. overt manipulation.

● *Appealing to People's Needs*

○ Identifying the desires and pain points of others.

○ Speaking to someone's self-interest to align your goals.

○ Using flattery without sounding disingenuous.

Section 2: Persuading in Professional Settings

● *Winning Over Clients or Colleagues*

○ How to build trust and rapport quickly in business.

○ Negotiation techniques that create win-win outcomes.

○ Navigating office politics with charm and tact.

● *The Elevator Pitch: Selling Yourself*

○ How to create a concise, compelling pitch that leaves an impact.

○ Highlighting your value in 60 seconds or less.

○ Tailoring your message to different audiences.

● *Presenting Your Ideas with Impact*

○ How to speak persuasively in meetings or presentations.

○ Engaging your audience with storytelling and data.

○ Addressing objections calmly and confidently.

Section 3: Persuasion in Social and Romantic Scenarios

- *Flirting Without Trying Too Hard*

○ How to show interest without appearing needy.

○ Reading romantic cues and responding with finesse.

○ Turning casual conversations into deeper connections.

- *Winning Over New Social Circles*

○ How to integrate smoothly into existing friend groups.

○ Becoming the person people naturally gravitate toward.

○ Balancing confidence with humility to build strong relationships.

- *The Art of Convincing Without Dominating*

○ How to lead conversations without overpowering others.

○ Persuading through listening and understanding.

○ Creating a sense of mutual respect and admiration.

Chapter 1: The Foundation of Charm – Building Unshakable Confidence

Confidence is often portrayed as a mysterious quality—something you either have or you don't. But in reality, confidence isn't an innate trait that a lucky few are born with. It's a skill that can be learned and developed over time, much like anything else. True confidence is not just about appearing poised and in control. It's about having a deep sense of self-assurance that comes from within, one that is unshakable regardless of the external circumstances. In this chapter, we'll explore the nature of confidence, why it plays a crucial role in charm, and how you can begin to build your own unshakable foundation.

Understanding Confidence

Let's start by addressing a common misconception: confidence and arrogance are not the same thing. Too often, people mistake arrogance—a superficial sense of superiority—for confidence, but the two are fundamentally different. Arrogance is a defense mechanism; it's a way of masking insecurities by projecting an exaggerated sense of self-worth. Confident people, on the other hand, don't need to put others down to feel good about themselves. They are secure in who they are, which allows them to lift others up, rather than stand above them.

Think of confidence as quiet strength. Imagine a time when you were in the presence of someone truly confident. Chances are, they weren't the loudest person in the room. They didn't dominate the conversation, nor did they constantly seek approval from those around them. Instead, they exuded a calm, self-assured energy that naturally drew people in. That's because true confidence isn't about demanding attention; it's about being comfortable in your own skin, no matter the situation.

This brings us to one of the most critical aspects of confidence: internal vs. external validation. Most people fall into the trap of seeking external validation—looking to others for approval, praise, or reassurance. When your sense of self-worth is tied to how others perceive you, your confidence becomes fragile. You'll constantly feel the need to prove yourself, and any criticism or rejection will shake your foundation.

True confidence, however, comes from within. It's rooted in a strong sense of self, independent of what others think or say. To build this kind of confidence, you must shift the focus away from external validation and start cultivating internal validation. This means taking ownership of your self-worth and recognizing that your value isn't determined by others' opinions. It's about knowing your strengths, embracing your flaws, and being okay with not pleasing everyone.

Confidence, at its core, is the bedrock of charm. Without it, any attempt at charm feels hollow, forced, or even manipulative. When you are confident, you don't have to try so hard. People are naturally drawn to those who are self-assured because they project a sense of stability and trustworthiness. If you can build this foundation, everything else—charm, charisma, influence—will flow more effortlessly.

Why People Are Attracted to Confidence

There's a reason confidence is universally attractive. Psychologically, we're wired to respond to confident individuals because they make us feel secure. Confidence signals competence, leadership, and reliability, all qualities that are highly valued in both social and professional settings. When someone is confident, it reassures others that they can be trusted, whether it's to lead a team, make important decisions, or simply hold a conversation.

One of the most fascinating aspects of confidence is how it influences social dynamics. People tend to mirror the energy of those around them. When you project confidence, others subconsciously pick up on that energy and respond in kind. This creates a ripple effect: your confidence boosts the confidence of those you interact with, making them feel more comfortable and engaged. This dynamic is why confident people often seem to "own" the room without having to say much. Their presence alone is enough to shift the energy of the space.

A key element of confidence is body language. Before you even open your mouth, your body is already communicating volumes about your confidence level. Are your shoulders slouched, or are they squared? Are you avoiding eye contact, or are you meeting people's gaze with ease? These subtle cues influence how others perceive you—and, more importantly, how you perceive yourself.

Take the example of an interview or a first date. In both situations, your body language plays a huge role in how the other person sees you. Imagine two different scenarios: In the first, you walk into the room with your head down, avoiding eye contact, and fidgeting with your hands. Even if you say all the right things, the lack of confidence in your body language undermines your message. In the second scenario, you walk in with your shoulders back, making direct eye contact, and offering a firm handshake. Before you've even spoken, you've already made a powerful impression. The same is true in everyday social interactions—how you carry yourself speaks louder than words.

Overcoming Self-Doubt

Now that we understand why confidence is so important, let's address one of the biggest obstacles to building it: self-doubt. Self-doubt is the nagging voice in your head that tells you you're not good enough, that you'll fail, or that others are judging you. It's that feeling of uncertainty that holds you back from taking risks, speaking up, or fully embracing opportunities.

The first step to overcoming self-doubt is recognizing that it's a universal experience. Even the most confident people face moments of self-doubt. The difference is that they don't let it control them. They've learned techniques for quieting that inner critic and moving forward despite their doubts.

One effective strategy is to reframe your past failures as growth opportunities. Too often, we let past mistakes define us, believing that our failures are a reflection of our worth. But the truth is, failure is one of the most valuable learning experiences we can have. Every time you fail, you gain new insights, develop resilience, and get one step closer to success. Confident people don't fear failure—they see it as a stepping stone toward growth.

Consider the story of Thomas Edison. When asked about the many failed attempts he made while inventing the lightbulb, he famously replied, "I have not failed. I've just found 10,000 ways that won't work." This mindset shift is crucial. Instead of viewing failure as something to be avoided, embrace it as part of the process. Each failure is an opportunity to learn, refine your approach, and ultimately succeed.

Another essential aspect of overcoming self-doubt is embracing vulnerability. Many people mistakenly believe that confidence means never showing weakness, but the opposite is true. True confidence is about being comfortable with your imperfections and being open about them. It's about recognizing that vulnerability is not a sign of weakness but a source of strength. When you allow yourself to be vulnerable, you invite deeper connections with others because it shows that you're authentic and relatable.

Think of it this way: Would you trust someone who acts like they have everything figured out and never admits to mistakes? Or would you feel more comfortable around someone who is honest about their struggles and willing to share their journey? Most people are drawn to the latter because vulnerability breeds trust and connection. When you stop trying to appear perfect and start embracing your flaws, you'll find that your confidence grows, and people are more naturally attracted to you.

In the end, building unshakable confidence isn't about pretending to be something you're not. It's about becoming more of who you already are—owning your strengths, learning from your weaknesses, and embracing your uniqueness. As you quiet the voice of self-doubt and cultivate your inner validation, you'll find that confidence becomes second nature. This newfound confidence will be the foundation upon which your charm, charisma, and influence are built. And as you continue through this book, you'll discover that with confidence, anything is possible.

Chapter 1: The Foundation of Charm – Building Unshakable Confidence

Section 2: Daily Confidence-Building Habits

True, lasting confidence doesn't appear overnight. It's not something you can simply turn on in the moment and expect to stay with you. Rather, confidence is built over time through consistent habits and intentional actions. By incorporating daily practices that strengthen your body, mind, and emotions, you create a solid foundation on which your confidence can grow. In this section, we'll explore how you can integrate confidence-building habits into your daily routine, from your first moments in the morning to your interactions throughout the day.

Morning Rituals for Success

How you start your day has a profound impact on your mood, energy, and ultimately, your confidence. Too often, we stumble into our mornings, scrolling through our phones or rushing to get ready, leaving little room for mental clarity or reflection. But what if you intentionally crafted a morning routine designed to set you up for success, both physically and mentally?

One of the most powerful tools for building confidence is the practice of **positive affirmations**. While it may sound simplistic, affirmations are an effective way to program your mind with empowering beliefs. When you *speak positively about yourself, you shift your* mindset from one of doubt to one of possibility. Consider the story of Muhammad Ali, one of the greatest boxers of

all the time. Long before he was recognized as the world champion, Ali would repeat to himself, "I am the greatest." He didn't wait for the world to affirm his greatness; he spoke it into existence.

You don't have to be a world-class athlete to benefit from affirmations. Each morning, take a moment to affirm the qualities you want to embody. For example, "I am confident, capable, and prepared to handle anything that comes my way." Speaking these words aloud may feel awkward at first, but over time, these affirmations will help you internalize the qualities you seek to cultivate. They set a positive tone for your day and serve as a reminder of your potential, especially when self-doubt creeps in.

In addition to affirmations, creating a **powerful morning routine** can significantly boost your confidence throughout the day. This doesn't have to be complicated. It could be as simple as waking up early, exercising, and spending a few quiet moments planning your day. The key is consistency. When you control the first hour of your day, you build momentum and a sense of accomplishment that carries you through the rest of your activities. Imagine starting each day with a small victory, like completing a quick workout or finishing a meditation session. These seemingly minor achievements stack up, reinforcing your belief in your ability to tackle bigger challenges.

Another essential part of a confidence-building morning routine is **visualization**. Athletes, entrepreneurs, and high achievers have long used visualization to mentally rehearse their success before it happens. Take a few minutes each morning to visualize yourself succeeding in your goals. See yourself walking into that important meeting with confidence, handling difficult conversations with ease, or presenting your ideas with authority. The more vividly you can imagine these scenarios, the more prepared you'll feel when they actually occur. Visualization primes your mind for success, reinforcing the belief that you are capable of achieving what you set out to do.

Body and Mind Connection

Confidence isn't just a mental game—it's deeply tied to your physical well-being. When your body feels strong and energized, it naturally supports a more confident state of mind. This is why physical fitness plays a crucial role in building confidence. It's not about becoming a fitness model; it's about cultivating a body that feels capable and resilient.

Consider the link between **physical fitness and mental clarity**. When you exercise regularly, you improve your mood, reduce stress, and boost your energy levels. All of these factors contribute to a more confident mindset. Think back to a time when you finished a workout or a run—how did you feel afterward? Chances are, you felt accomplished, invigorated, and more capable of handling whatever came your way. That post-workout rush isn't just about endorphins; it's a reflection of the confidence that comes from knowing you've invested in your health and well-being.

To further enhance this body-mind connection, incorporate **breathing exercises** into your daily routine. In moments of stress or anxiety, your breath is one of the most powerful tools you have to regain control and calm yourself. Slow, deep breathing signals to your brain that you are safe, helping to lower your heart rate and reduce feelings of panic. Practicing deep breathing, even for a few minutes each day, can build your ability to stay calm under pressure, whether you're giving a presentation, negotiating a deal, or navigating a tense social situation.

Consider the link between **physical fitness and mental clarity**. When you exercise regularly, you improve your mood, reduce stress, and boost your energy levels. All of these factors contribute to a more confident mindset. Think back to a time when you finished a workout or a run—how did you feel afterward? Chances are, you felt accomplished, invigorated, and more capable of handling whatever came your way. That post-workout rush isn't just about endorphins; it's a reflection of the confidence that comes from knowing you've invested in your health and well-being.

To further enhance this body-mind connection, incorporate **breathing exercises** into your daily routine. In moments of stress or anxiety, your breath is one of the most powerful tools you have to regain control and calm yourself. Slow, deep breathing signals to your brain that you are safe, helping to lower your heart rate and reduce feelings of panic. Practicing deep breathing, even for a few minutes each day, can build your ability to stay calm under pressure, whether you're giving a presentation, negotiating a deal, or navigating a tense social situation.

Another tool that can dramatically impact your confidence is **meditation and mindfulness**. These practices teach you to quiet the mental chatter and focus on the present moment. When you meditate regularly, you build emotional control and resilience, which directly translates into confidence. The next time you're faced with a challenging situation, you'll notice that your mind is clearer and more focused, allowing you to respond thoughtfully instead of reacting impulsively.

In a world where distractions are constant, developing the habit of mindfulness helps you stay grounded and centered. It's easy to get caught up in worries about the future or regrets about the past, but mindfulness teaches you to be fully present in the moment. When you are present, you are more aware of your body language, tone of voice, and the energy you're projecting—all crucial aspects of confidence.

The Power of Preparation

While daily rituals like affirmations, exercise, and mindfulness lay the foundation for confidence, one of the most practical ways to boost your confidence is through **preparation**. Confidence doesn't come from winging it—it comes from knowing you're ready for whatever comes your way. Preparation gives you an undeniable edge in any situation, from social interactions to professional settings.

Take, for example, the difference between two speakers. The first speaker walks into a presentation unprepared, hoping that they can rely on their natural charisma to carry them through. As soon as they encounter a difficult question or unexpected technical issue, their confidence crumbles. The second speaker, however, has spent time researching their audience, practicing their delivery, and anticipating potential challenges. Even if things go wrong, they're able to adapt and recover because they are prepared. This second speaker's confidence isn't a product of luck—it's a result of diligent preparation.

The power of preparation also extends to seemingly small, everyday situations. For example, if you're attending a networking event or social gathering, take a few moments to think about the people you might meet and the topics you can discuss. By having a mental script of potential conversation starters or questions, you'll feel more at ease and ready to engage. This simple step of preparation can make all the difference in how confident you feel during the event.

Building unshakable confidence is not a one-time achievement but a daily practice. By incorporating habits like morning affirmations, regular exercise, mindfulness, and thoughtful preparation, you create a solid foundation of confidence that will carry you through even the most challenging situations. These habits not only strengthen your belief in yourself but also project an aura of confidence that others will naturally gravitate toward. Over time, you'll find that confidence becomes second nature, allowing you to approach life with greater ease, charm, and success.

Chapter 1: The Foundation of Charm – Building Unshakable Confidence

Section 3: Projecting Confidence to Others

Confidence is not just an internal experience; it's something that people feel and respond to when they interact with you. True confidence doesn't come from boasting or bravado, but rather from a quiet assurance in yourself that is projected through your body language, the way you communicate, and how you carry yourself. This section will explore the art of projecting confidence to others, transforming the internal belief into an external reality that others can see, feel, and respect.

Mastering Body Language

The way you carry yourself physically is the first thing people notice about you, often before you've even had the chance to speak. Body language is the silent ambassador of confidence—it speaks volumes without saying a word. But it's not about exaggerating movements or trying to dominate a room; instead, it's about demonstrating control, ease, and self-assuredness in a natural, compelling way.

One of the most critical aspects of confident body language is **posture**. Imagine walking into a room for an important meeting. If your shoulders are hunched, your eyes are downcast, and your movements are hesitant, people will read that energy instantly. On the other hand, when you stand tall, with your shoulders back, and your head held high, you project a sense of command and control. This doesn't mean rigidly stiffening your body, but rather, aligning it in a way that signals you are grounded and sure of yourself. There's a reason military personnel are trained to stand at attention: posture creates an immediate impression of confidence and authority.

Consider the story of Tony, a young professional who often struggled with social anxiety. At networking events, Tony found himself shrinking away from conversations, avoiding eye contact, and nervously fidgeting. Over time, he learned that by simply adjusting his posture—standing up straight, relaxing his hands, and making deliberate eye contact—he began to feel more confident. It wasn't an overnight transformation, but as his posture improved, so did the way people responded to him. They began to engage with him more easily, sensing his newfound assurance.

Another key element of body language is **eye contact**. Eye contact is powerful—it conveys trust, interest, and authority. When you hold someone's gaze, you're sending a signal that you're fully present and engaged. However, there's a fine line between making confident eye contact and making someone uncomfortable by staring too intensely. The goal is to strike a balance: hold eye contact for a few seconds, then break it naturally and look elsewhere. This rhythm helps build rapport and makes others feel seen and heard.

Think about influential leaders, speakers, or even actors who capture attention effortlessly. Their eye contact isn't fleeting or uncertain—it's steady and intentional. By using eye contact as a tool, you not only assert confidence but also create a connection with the person or people you're interacting with.

Of course, first impressions are often shaped by the very first physical interaction—**the handshake**. A handshake says a lot about your confidence level. Too weak, and you may come across as unsure of yourself. Too firm, and you risk overpowering the other person. The ideal handshake is one that's firm but not crushing, confident but not forceful. It's a subtle gesture, but it speaks volumes about how you perceive yourself and how you want others to perceive you. When shaking hands, make sure to maintain eye contact and offer a warm smile—this combination exudes confidence without needing to say a word.

Conversational Confidence

Projecting confidence isn't just about how you move or hold yourself, but how you communicate. Your words, tone, and delivery all contribute to the impression you make on others. The key to **conversational confidence** is finding the balance between speaking clearly and assertively, while also knowing when to listen.

Many people mistake confidence for dominating a conversation, but in reality, confident individuals understand that communication is a two-way street. Think about a time when you were in a conversation with someone who monopolized the discussion, leaving little room for others to contribute. It likely left you feeling unheard and unimportant. In contrast, those who balance speaking with active listening come across as more confident because they demonstrate a calm assurance in themselves and don't feel the need to constantly prove their worth through words.

When you speak, **clarity and assertiveness** are your best allies. Confidence is not about raising your voice or overpowering others, but rather about delivering your message with certainty. Take the example of Sarah, a project manager who used to struggle with speaking up in meetings. She often doubted whether her contributions were valuable, leading her to speak hesitantly or apologize for her ideas before even expressing them. After working on speaking with clarity and conviction, Sarah noticed a dramatic shift in how her colleagues responded to her. By simply stating her ideas clearly and without unnecessary qualifiers ("I think, maybe, possibly..."), she gained respect and attention in the room.

At the same time, confident people know when to **listen**. Listening actively doesn't just mean waiting for your turn to speak—it means fully engaging with the other person's words, asking thoughtful questions, and responding in a way that shows you've understood their point. When you listen deeply, you show that you're secure enough in yourself to let others take the spotlight for a while. This creates an environment of mutual respect and fosters stronger connections.

But what happens when conversations take a negative turn? **Dealing with criticism** is one of the ultimate tests of confidence. It's easy to remain poised when the feedback is positive, but when faced with critique or disagreement, many people become defensive or shut down. A confident person, however, welcomes feedback—even if it's difficult to hear. They don't see criticism as a personal attack, but as an opportunity for growth. Picture a scenario where you're given negative feedback at work. Instead of getting defensive or making excuses, a confident approach would be to calmly acknowledge the feedback, ask clarifying questions if needed, and express a willingness to improve. This response not only diffuses tension but also demonstrates maturity and emotional intelligence.

Owning Your Presence

Beyond body language and communication, projecting confidence also involves how you carry yourself in various environments—whether that's walking into a room, engaging a group of people, or handling mistakes. **Owning your presence** means taking up space with purpose and authority, without shrinking or hesitating.

Consider the moment when you walk into a room full of strangers, whether it's a party, a networking event, or a meeting. For many, this can be an intimidating situation, leading them to hover near the door or avoid making eye contact. However, confident individuals enter a room with **purpose**. They walk in with their head high, shoulders back, and a sense of direction. They don't hesitate or second-guess themselves. This commanding presence sets the tone for how others perceive them. It's the difference between someone who blends into the background and someone who immediately captures attention.

When engaging a group of people, confidence is contagious. A confident person speaks with **energy and enthusiasm**, drawing people in with their passion and conviction. Think of charismatic speakers who can hold an audience's attention for hours. It's not just their words—it's their energy. They're fully present, fully engaged, and it shows. This doesn't mean you need to become an extroverted entertainer, but rather, that you bring your full self to the moment. When you're genuinely invested in what you're saying and doing, people naturally gravitate toward you.

Finally, one of the most underrated aspects of confidence is how you handle **mistakes**. No one is perfect, and confident people understand that mistakes are inevitable. Instead of trying to cover up errors or beat themselves up over them, they **own their mistakes**. They acknowledge when something has gone wrong, take responsibility, and learn from the experience. Think of the entrepreneur who admits to a failed business venture not with embarrassment, but with pride in the lessons learned. By turning failure into a tool for growth, confident people show that their self-worth isn't tied to perfection, but to resilience and the ability to bounce back stronger.

Projecting confidence to others is an art that requires self-awareness, practice, and a willingness to step outside of your comfort zone. By mastering your body language, speaking with clarity and conviction, and owning your presence in any environment, you can create a lasting impression of confidence that others will respond to positively. Confidence isn't about perfection—it's about showing up fully, embracing who you are, and handling whatever comes your way with grace and assurance. Over time, as these habits become second nature, you'll find that confidence flows naturally, allowing you to navigate the world with greater ease and impact.

Chapter 2: Mastering the First Impression – How to Make Every Interaction Count

Section 1: The Psychology of First Impressions

The concept of a first impression is deceptively simple: it's that initial judgment people form about you in the first few seconds of meeting. Yet, its significance is profound, often setting the tone for the entire relationship that follows. This section delves into why first impressions matter so much, explores the concept of the Halo Effect, and offers practical advice on creating a memorable introduction. By understanding the psychology behind these early interactions, you can master the art of making every first impression count.

Why First Impressions Matter

Imagine walking into a room full of strangers. Within moments, people are forming opinions about you based on your appearance, body language, and the way you carry yourself. This is not just a superficial process but a deeply ingrained psychological response. **The science behind how we form judgments within seconds** reveals that humans are wired to make quick assessments as a survival mechanism. These initial judgments are based on visible cues and can heavily influence how we're perceived in the long term.

The speed at which we form these judgments is astonishing. According to psychological research, it takes less than one-tenth of a second for someone to form an impression of your trustworthiness. This means that your initial appearance and behavior are crucial in determining whether people see you as credible, likable, or competent. If you're trying to make a positive impact—whether at a job interview, a networking event, or a social gathering—these first moments are your opportunity to set the stage for future interactions.

However, the importance of first impressions extends beyond mere introductions. **How these judgments impact long-term relationships** can be profound. Studies show that people are likely to stick with their initial impressions, even in the face of contradictory evidence. If your first impression is positive, it can create a favorable foundation that makes it easier to build trust and rapport. Conversely, a negative first impression can be a hurdle that's difficult to overcome, even if you subsequently demonstrate competence and likability.

But what if your first impression doesn't go as planned? **Overcoming negative first impressions** requires more than just a quick recovery. It often involves demonstrating your qualities consistently over time to counteract initial misjudgments. For example, if you inadvertently come across as aloof in a social setting, actively engaging in subsequent interactions and showing genuine interest in others can gradually shift perceptions. It's about proving through your actions that the initial impression was not a true reflection of who you are.

The Halo Effect

One of the most intriguing aspects of first impressions is the concept of the **Halo Effect**. This psychological phenomenon occurs when one positive attribute of a person leads to an overall favorable impression. For instance, if someone is perceived as attractive, they are often assumed to possess other positive qualities, such as intelligence and kindness, even if there's no direct evidence to support this.

Understanding the Halo Effect allows you to **use it to your advantage**. When meeting someone for the first time, your appearance, demeanor, and initial interactions can create a halo that influences how all your other attributes are perceived. For example, if you dress sharply and present yourself confidently, people are more likely to assume you are competent and reliable. This initial positive perception can pave the way for more favorable evaluations of your subsequent behavior and performance.

Appearing well-rounded is another way to leverage the Halo Effect. When you showcase a blend of traits—such as confidence, competence, and approachability—you create a multi-dimensional impression that can elevate your charm. Think of influential public figures like Steve Jobs, who was known not only for his innovative genius but also for his charismatic presentations and polished image. His overall persona created a powerful halo effect that made people more receptive to his ideas and vision.

Examples of people using the Halo Effect effectively abound in the public sphere. Take Oprah Winfrey, for instance. Her warmth and authenticity in media appearances created a halo effect that extended beyond her on-screen persona, leading to widespread trust and admiration. By consistently demonstrating these qualities, she built an image of a compassionate, insightful leader. This halo effect has been instrumental in her success, from her talk show to her ventures in publishing and philanthropy.

Creating a Memorable Introduction

Crafting a **memorable introduction** is both an art and a strategic move. When you introduce yourself, you have a brief window to make an impact that sets the tone for the rest of the interaction. The goal is to leave a lasting impression that reflects your personality and strengths.

The art of the perfect introduction involves more than just stating your name and title. It's about conveying who you are in a way that resonates with the listener. For instance, instead of saying, "Hi, I'm Alex. I work in marketing," you might say, "Hi, I'm Alex. I help brands tell their stories in a way that connects with people's emotions." The latter introduction not only provides information about your role but also gives a glimpse into your passion and approach.

Shaping your personal brand through your introduction means aligning it with the qualities you want to be known for. If you're aiming to be seen as innovative and forward-thinking, frame your introduction to highlight those aspects. It's about creating a cohesive narrative that reflects your unique value proposition. For example, if you're meeting a potential client, you might introduce yourself with a focus on how you solve problems or bring new ideas to the table, rather than just listing your credentials.

Using humor and curiosity can also make your introduction stand out. Humor, when used appropriately, can break the ice and make you more approachable. It can be as simple as sharing a light-hearted anecdote related to your field or a playful observation about the situation. Curiosity, on the other hand, involves showing genuine interest in the other person. Asking engaging questions not only demonstrates your interest but also helps establish a connection. For example, after introducing yourself, you might ask, "What brought you to this event?" or "What's the most exciting project you're working on right now?" This approach turns the introduction into a two-way conversation and sets the stage for a meaningful exchange.

By mastering these elements of first impressions—understanding their importance, leveraging the Halo Effect, and crafting a memorable introduction—you position yourself to make a strong, positive impact from the very start. These skills are essential not just for social interactions, but for any scenario where establishing a favorable impression can lead to greater opportunities and stronger relationships. As you refine these techniques, you'll find that you're not just making a good impression—you're setting the stage for successful, enduring connections.

Chapter 2: Mastering the First Impression – How to Make Every Interaction Count

Section 2: Dressing for Success

When it comes to making a memorable first impression, the adage "dress for success" couldn't be more accurate. Your clothing choices do more than just cover your body; they communicate your personality, confidence, and attention to detail. This section delves into how your style reflects your inner confidence, offers practical grooming advice, and provides insights into dressing appropriately for various occasions. By understanding the impact of your attire and grooming habits, you can enhance your charm and make every interaction count.

Style as a Reflection of Inner Confidence

Imagine walking into a room where everyone is dressed in polished, well-fitting outfits that reflect their personal style and confidence. Now, picture someone entering in clothes that seem ill-fitting or out of place. The difference in perception is immediate and significant. Your clothing doesn't merely cover you; it sends a powerful message about who you are and how you perceive yourself.

How your clothes communicate personality and confidence is evident in the way people respond to you. When you wear clothes that fit well and align with your personal style, you project an image of self-assurance. Take, for example, the story of Emma, a young professional who was known for her impeccable style. Emma wasn't necessarily following the latest fashion trends; rather, she had curated a wardrobe that suited her personality and career ambitions. Her tailored blazers and well-chosen accessories spoke volumes about her professionalism and attention to detail. As a result, her colleagues and clients perceived her as someone who took her work seriously and carried herself with confidence.

Building a wardrobe that matches your lifestyle and ambitions involves more than just purchasing the latest styles. It's about curating pieces that resonate with your personal brand and the image you wish to project. If you're an entrepreneur aiming to convey innovation and creativity, your wardrobe might include unique patterns or statement pieces that reflect this ethos. On the other hand, if you work in a more traditional industry, such as finance or law, a classic, tailored wardrobe might be more appropriate. The key is to choose clothing that not only fits your current role but also aligns with where you aspire to go. This thoughtful approach ensures that your style evolves with you, supporting your journey rather than merely following fleeting trends.

Why fit, color, and attention to detail matter can't be overstated. Ill-fitting clothes, no matter how expensive or stylish, can detract from your overall appearance. Conversely, well-fitted garments enhance your silhouette and project an image of self-respect and care. Color choices also play a crucial role; certain colors can evoke specific emotions or associations. For instance, a navy suit exudes professionalism and reliability, while a vibrant tie might signal creativity and confidence. Attention to detail, such as well-polished shoes or a neatly pressed shirt, further demonstrates that you pay attention to the nuances of your appearance, which often translates into how you approach your work and relationships.

The Suave Man's Guide to Grooming

Grooming is the subtle art of refining your appearance to complement your personal style and enhance your confidence. While clothing sets the stage, grooming provides the finishing touches that complete your overall look.

Daily grooming habits that make a difference are the small, consistent practices that contribute to a polished appearance. This doesn't require an elaborate routine, but rather a commitment to regular maintenance. For example, maintaining a well-trimmed beard or neatly shaven face, keeping your hair styled and clean, and ensuring that your nails are trimmed and clean all contribute to a well-groomed appearance. Consider the case of Alex, who found that investing a few extra minutes each day in his grooming routine significantly impacted how he was perceived. By adopting a daily regimen that included proper skincare, haircuts, and beard maintenance, Alex noticed an improvement in his confidence and the way others responded to him.

Subtle details: scent, hair, and accessories can make a lasting impression. A signature scent, while not overpowering, can evoke a sense of familiarity and elegance. Choose a fragrance that complements your personality and leaves a subtle trail without being overwhelming. Hair maintenance is equally important; a well-cut and styled haircut contributes to a clean and professional look. Accessories, such as a classic watch or a well-chosen tie, can enhance your outfit without overshadowing it. Think of someone like James Bond, whose impeccably groomed appearance and refined accessories are as much a part of his charm as his suave demeanor.

Creating a **signature look** involves selecting and refining elements that become synonymous with your personal style. This might mean investing in a few high-quality, versatile pieces that you wear frequently and that reflect your unique taste. For instance, if you have a penchant for tailored suits, find a style that complements your body type and personal flair. Over time, this consistent style becomes a defining feature of your personal brand, contributing to a coherent and memorable image.

Dressing for the Occasion

The ability to dress appropriately for various occasions is a critical aspect of projecting confidence and charm. The right attire not only demonstrates your understanding of social norms but also ensures that you're comfortable and self-assured in any setting.

The importance of dressing appropriately for the situation cannot be underestimated. Wearing the right outfit for an occasion shows respect for the event and its participants. For example, arriving at a formal business meeting in a casual outfit can undermine your credibility, while overdressing for a casual gathering might come across as pretentious. Consider the example of Rachel, who always made it a point to research the dress code for events she attended. By dressing appropriately, she communicated that she valued the occasion and was considerate of the setting, which in turn enhanced her rapport with others.

How to look effortless in both formal and casual settings involves understanding the nuances of different dress codes. For formal events, such as weddings or high-level business meetings, classic attire like a well-tailored suit or elegant dress is appropriate. The key is to look polished and sophisticated without appearing overly rigid. For casual settings, such as social gatherings or informal work environments, aim for a look that is relaxed yet put-together. This might mean opting for well-fitted jeans and a stylish shirt or a smart casual dress. The goal is to strike a balance between looking effortless and maintaining a sense of style and appropriateness.

Navigating tricky dress codes with confidence requires a blend of knowledge and adaptability. When faced with ambiguous or non-standard dress codes, it's helpful to err on the side of slightly more formal or classic choices. If you're unsure about a dress code like "business casual," choosing a smart blazer, tailored trousers, and a crisp shirt can ensure that you're appropriately dressed without appearing overdressed. Additionally, seeking clarification from the event organizer or reviewing dress code guidelines online can provide valuable insight and help you make an informed decision.

Dressing for success is about more than just following trends; it's about aligning your clothing choices with your personal brand and the context of each interaction. By understanding how your style reflects your inner confidence, maintaining thoughtful grooming habits, and dressing appropriately for various occasions, you create a powerful first impression that supports your charm and effectiveness in any setting. When your appearance is intentional and well-considered, it enhances your overall presence and sets the stage for positive, impactful interactions.

Chapter 2: Mastering the First Impression – How to Make Every Interaction Count

Section 3: Nonverbal Communication

In the delicate dance of first impressions, nonverbal communication plays a pivotal role. It's often said that actions speak louder than words, and when it comes to making a strong first impression, this rings particularly true. Nonverbal cues—body language, gestures, facial expressions, and the artful use of pauses—can significantly influence how you are perceived. This section explores how to read the room, effectively use gestures and expressions, and harness the power of strategic pauses to enhance your interactions.

How to Read the Room

Understanding the social dynamics of a room starts with observing body language cues. Imagine walking into a networking event filled with professionals. At first glance, you might notice clusters of people engaged in animated conversations, while others stand alone or appear less involved. This initial scan can offer valuable insights into the social climate and help you navigate the room more effectively.

Observing body language cues to gauge the social climate involves paying attention to how people position themselves and interact with others. For example, if you see a group with open stances, relaxed body language, and frequent eye contact, it indicates a welcoming and engaging environment. Conversely, crossed arms, minimal eye contact, or physical distancing might signal discomfort or disinterest. By tuning into these signals, you can adjust your approach to fit the prevailing mood. Take John, who frequently attended industry conferences. John's ability to read the room was one of his strongest assets. At a recent event, he noticed that while most people were clustered in lively groups, a few individuals stood apart, looking uncomfortable. Instead of joining the larger groups, John approached those who seemed isolated, engaging them in conversation with genuine curiosity. His ability to adapt based on the social climate not only helped him forge meaningful connections but also earned him a reputation as someone who truly valued others' perspectives.

Picking up on subtle signs of interest or disengagement is also crucial. In a conversation, subtle cues like nodding, leaning in, or mirroring your posture often indicate engagement and interest. On the other hand, looking away, checking the time, or crossing arms can suggest disinterest or discomfort. For instance, during a pitch meeting, if you notice your audience's eyes glazing over or their bodies shifting away, it might be time to adjust your presentation or pivot to a more engaging topic. Being attuned to these signals allows you to make real-time adjustments and maintain a positive connection.

Using Gestures and Facial Expressions

Gestures and facial expressions are powerful tools in nonverbal communication, often conveying more than words ever could. **How to use open gestures to build rapport** involves employing body language that invites engagement and fosters a sense of openness. For example, keeping your hands visible and using open gestures, like spreading your arms slightly when speaking, can make you appear more approachable and trustworthy.

Consider a scenario where you're giving a presentation. By using expansive hand gestures and maintaining an open stance, you convey confidence and enthusiasm, making your audience more likely to respond positively. The key is to ensure that your gestures are natural and in sync with your message. Overly dramatic gestures might come off as insincere, while too little movement can make you appear rigid. Finding the right balance is crucial for effective communication.

Smiling with authenticity is another critical aspect of nonverbal communication. A genuine smile, which involves the eyes as well as the mouth, is universally recognized as a sign of friendliness and warmth. For example, during a job interview, a natural, sincere smile can make you appear more approachable and likable. Authentic smiles can help diffuse tension, build rapport, and create a more positive interaction. Practice smiling in front of a mirror to ensure it feels natural and reflects your true emotions.

Mirroring techniques can further enhance your ability to connect with others. Mirroring involves subtly mimicking the other person's body language, such as adopting a similar posture or repeating their gestures. This technique can help build instant connections and create a sense of empathy. For example, if you're in a conversation and notice the other person leaning slightly forward, you might do the same. This subtle alignment can make them feel understood and valued, strengthening the rapport between you.

The Art of the Pause

Mastering the **art of the pause** can greatly enhance your communication skills, creating impact and intrigue. Strategic pauses, whether in conversation or during a presentation, can help emphasize key points and give your audience time to absorb your message. For instance, during a public speaking engagement, pausing just before delivering a crucial statement can build anticipation and underscore the importance of what you're about to say.

Avoiding **verbal fillers** like "um" or "like" is essential for maintaining a poised and confident demeanor. Verbal fillers can undermine your credibility and make you appear less assured. Practice replacing these fillers with pauses, which not only sound more polished but also give you a moment to gather your thoughts. For example, if you're explaining a complex concept, a well-timed pause can enhance clarity and give your audience time to process the information.

Pausing to listen is equally important for building trust and attentiveness. When you allow for pauses in conversations, it demonstrates that you value the other person's input and are genuinely interested in what they have to say. This practice not only fosters deeper connections but also encourages more meaningful exchanges. Consider a situation where you're in a dialogue with a client. By actively listening and pausing before responding, you show respect for their perspective and give thoughtful, well-considered replies. This attentiveness can significantly enhance your rapport and effectiveness in communication.

Mastering nonverbal communication is about more than just adopting the right body language or gestures; it's about being attuned to the subtle signals of those around you and using your own nonverbal cues to build genuine connections. By learning to read the room, effectively use gestures and facial expressions, and harness the power of strategic pauses, you can enhance your ability to make a memorable first impression and foster positive interactions. These skills not only improve how you're perceived but also enable you to navigate social and professional settings with greater ease and confidence.

Chapter 3: The Suave Conversationalist – Navigating Any Social Situation with Ease

Section 1: The Science of Great Conversations

Mastering the art of conversation is an essential skill for anyone looking to elevate their social interactions and professional networking. Great conversations aren't just about exchanging words; they involve a deeper understanding of the people you're interacting with, the ability to read between the lines, and the skillful use of storytelling. This section delves into the science behind effective conversations, focusing on active listening, asking the right questions, and the power of storytelling.

Active Listening

At the heart of every meaningful conversation is active listening. This goes beyond merely hearing the words spoken; it's about engaging with the speaker on a deeper level, absorbing their message, and responding in a way that shows genuine understanding.

Techniques to truly listen and understand, not just respond, involve several key practices. Start by giving the speaker your full attention. This means putting away distractions, like your phone, and focusing entirely on the person in front of you. Maintain eye contact and use nonverbal cues like nodding or leaning slightly forward to show that you're engaged. For instance, when Samantha, a project manager, engaged with her team during meetings, she made a habit of summarizing key points and reflecting back on what was said. This practice not only confirmed her understanding but also made her team feel heard and valued.

How listening boosts your likability and charm can't be understated. When people feel genuinely listened to, they're more likely to view you as approachable and empathetic. This effect is often seen in high-stakes situations, such as job interviews. For example, Alex, a hiring manager, found that candidates who actively listened and engaged in thoughtful conversation were perceived more favorably. Their ability to listen attentively and respond with relevant questions or comments demonstrated their interest and respect, making them stand out as candidates.

Reading between the lines: Picking up on what's unsaid is another crucial aspect of active listening. Not everything is communicated verbally; body language, tone of voice, and facial expressions often provide additional context. For instance, if someone says, "I'm fine," but their tone is flat and their posture is closed off, it may indicate underlying issues or discomfort. Being attuned to these subtleties allows you to respond more empathetically and effectively. During a team meeting, if a colleague's verbal reassurance doesn't align with their nonverbal cues, addressing the unspoken concerns can lead to more productive and supportive conversations.

Asking the Right Questions

The questions you ask in a conversation can steer its direction and depth. How to ask open-ended questions that spark deeper conversation involves framing your questions in a way that encourages expansive responses. Open-ended questions, such as "What inspired you to pursue this career?" or "How do you envision the future of this project?" invite the other person to share their thoughts, experiences, and feelings in greater detail. This approach not only fosters richer dialogue but also reveals more about the speaker, allowing for more meaningful interactions.

Using curiosity to make others feel valued is a powerful conversational tool. When you ask questions driven by genuine curiosity, it shows that you're interested in the other person's perspective and experiences. For instance, when Jane met a new client, she made it a point to ask about their background, interests, and goals. Her curiosity wasn't just about gathering information; it was about making the client feel valued and understood. This approach helped build a strong rapport and set the stage for a successful business relationship.

Balancing conversation: When to speak and when to listen is key to maintaining a dynamic and engaging dialogue. A common pitfall is dominating the conversation or, conversely, not contributing enough. Aim for a balanced exchange where both parties have the opportunity to share and respond. For example, during a social gathering, if you find yourself speaking more than listening, take a step back and ask the other person about their experiences or opinions. This balance ensures that the conversation remains engaging and inclusive, fostering a more enjoyable and meaningful interaction for everyone involved.

The Power of Storytelling

Storytelling is a compelling tool in conversations, allowing you to connect with others on an emotional level and leave a lasting impression. Why stories are a powerful tool for connection lies in their ability to evoke emotions and create shared experiences. A well-told story can captivate your audience, making your message more memorable and engaging. For example, during a networking event, sharing a personal story about overcoming a challenge or achieving a goal can resonate with others, providing a glimpse into your character and values.

How to share personal anecdotes without oversharing involves striking a balance between revealing enough to connect and maintaining appropriate boundaries. When sharing stories, focus on experiences that are relevant to the conversation and avoid delving into overly personal or sensitive topics. For instance, if you're discussing career development with a colleague, sharing a story about a professional challenge and how you overcame it can provide valuable insights without crossing personal boundaries. The key is to be mindful of the context and the comfort level of your audience.

Building emotional resonance through compelling narratives requires crafting stories that are both relatable and impactful. Use vivid details, emotions, and reflections to bring your story to life. For example, when describing a project you're passionate about, detail the challenges you faced, the emotions you experienced, and the ultimate outcome. This approach not only engages your audience but also helps them connect with your experiences on a deeper level. The goal is to create a narrative that resonates with others and fosters a sense of shared understanding.

Mastering the science of great conversations involves more than just exchanging pleasantries; it requires a deep understanding of active listening, effective questioning, and the art of storytelling. By honing these skills, you can navigate social situations with ease, build meaningful connections, and enhance your overall charm and likability. Whether you're in a professional setting or a casual social gathering, the ability to engage thoughtfully and empathetic with others will leave a lasting impression and elevate your conversational prowess.

Chapter 3: The Suave Conversationalist – Navigating Any Social Situation with Ease

Section 2: Navigating Difficult Conversations

Navigating difficult conversations with grace is an art form that distinguishes the suave conversationalist from the average communicator. Whether you're facing a heated discussion, handling criticism, or setting boundaries, your approach can either defuse tension or escalate conflict. This section explores practical strategies for staying cool under pressure, dealing with criticism gracefully, and maintaining boundaries while preserving your charm.

Staying Cool Under Pressure

In the heat of a contentious discussion, maintaining composure is crucial. **Techniques to stay calm in heated discussions** involve a combination of mental and physical strategies. One effective method is to practice deep breathing. When you find yourself becoming agitated, take a moment to breathe deeply and slowly. This simple act can help reduce stress and provide a momentary pause to collect your thoughts.

Consider a situation where Sarah, a team leader, had to address a conflict between two employees. The discussion quickly escalated, with both parties raising their voices. Instead of joining in the escalation, Sarah took a deep breath and calmly acknowledged each person's viewpoint. Her composed demeanor helped to de-escalate the situation, turning it from a heated argument into a constructive dialogue. By staying calm and focusing on understanding both sides, Sarah was able to facilitate a resolution and maintain her professional charm.

Turning confrontation into productive dialogue requires a shift in perspective. Instead of viewing confrontation as a personal attack, approach it as an opportunity for growth and problem-solving. For example, if you're in a disagreement with a colleague, reframe the conversation by focusing on finding a solution rather than defending your position. By adopting a collaborative mindset, you can transform potential conflict into a productive exchange of ideas.

How to respectfully disagree while maintaining charm involves a delicate balance. When expressing a differing opinion, do so with tact and empathy. For instance, if a friend makes a comment that you disagree with, you might say, "I see where you're coming from, but I have a different perspective." This approach acknowledges their viewpoint while gently introducing your own, fostering a respectful and constructive conversation.

Dealing with Criticism Gracefully

Criticism, whether constructive or otherwise, can be challenging to handle. **How to accept feedback without getting defensive** involves adopting a mindset of openness and curiosity. When receiving criticism, listen actively and avoid interrupting. For example, during a performance review, instead of reacting defensively to feedback, focus on understanding the underlying concerns and ask clarifying questions. This approach demonstrates maturity and a willingness to improve.

Using criticism as a tool for growth and improvement requires viewing feedback as an opportunity rather than a setback. Reflect on the critique and identify actionable steps for improvement. For instance, if a colleague points out areas for development in your work, take note of their suggestions and create a plan to address them. By embracing criticism as a chance to enhance your skills, you can turn potentially negative experiences into valuable learning opportunities.

Responding to insults with class and composure is another critical aspect of handling difficult conversations. When faced with personal attacks, maintain your dignity by refusing to engage in reciprocal negativity. For example, if someone insults you during a heated discussion, respond with a calm and measured tone, such as, "I prefer to focus on the issue at hand rather than personal remarks." This response not only defuses the situation but also reinforces your composure and grace under pressure.

Keeping Boundaries While Staying Suave

Maintaining boundaries while remaining charming involves a combination of assertiveness and diplomacy. **How to assert yourself without being aggressive** requires clear communication and self-awareness. When expressing your needs or limits, do so confidently but with respect. For example, if you're overwhelmed with work and need to decline additional responsibilities, you might say, "I'm currently at full capacity with my existing projects, so I won't be able to take on additional tasks at this time." This approach communicates your boundaries while maintaining a professional and courteous tone.

Politely saying "no" while protecting your time and energy involves setting clear limits without feeling guilty. It's important to recognize that saying no is a necessary aspect of managing your time and maintaining your well-being. For instance, if a friend invites you to an event that conflicts with your personal time, respond with, "I appreciate the invitation, but I need to take some time for myself this weekend." By being honest about your priorities, you can maintain your boundaries while preserving your relationships.

Maintaining boundaries in professional and social settings requires consistency and self-respect. In professional environments, clearly define your limits regarding work hours, tasks, and responsibilities. For example, if a colleague frequently interrupts your work time with non-urgent requests, set boundaries by stating, "I'm currently focused on a project, but I'm happy to address any issues after 3 PM." In social settings, communicate your boundaries with kindness and firmness, ensuring that your needs are respected without alienating others.

Navigating difficult conversations with poise is a hallmark of a suave conversationalist. By mastering the art of staying cool under pressure, handling criticism gracefully, and maintaining boundaries with respect and clarity, you can turn challenging interactions into opportunities for growth and positive connection. These skills not only enhance your ability to manage conflict but also contribute to a more polished and charming presence in any social or professional setting.

Chapter 3: Mastering the First Impression – How to Make Every Interaction Count

Section 3: Becoming a Social Chameleon

In the world of social interactions, being a "social chameleon" means seamlessly adapting to various environments and personalities while leaving a memorable impression. This skill is crucial for navigating diverse social settings, from high-stakes boardrooms to casual bars. It involves not just adjusting your demeanor but also mastering the art of rapport-building and leaving a lasting impression. Let's explore how to become a social chameleon and make every interaction count.

Adapting to Different Social Environments

The ability to adapt to different social environments is essential for making a positive impression. Whether you're stepping into a formal boardroom or mingling at a lively bar, your ability to adjust your approach can significantly impact how you're perceived.

How to be at ease in any situation, from boardrooms to bars starts with understanding the context and the people you'll be interacting with. For example, when Jake, a senior executive, attended a high-profile business dinner, he knew the atmosphere would be formal and serious. He dressed in a sharp suit, maintained a professional tone, and focused on discussing industry trends and strategic insights. Conversely, at a casual networking event, Jake opted for a more relaxed outfit and engaged in lighter, more personal conversations. By tailoring his approach to fit the setting, he was able to connect effectively with different audiences.

Adjusting your style of conversation to fit the setting involves modifying your language and topics based on the environment. In a boardroom, you might use industry jargon and focus on strategic goals, whereas in a bar, a more informal, conversational style might be appropriate. For instance, during a company retreat, Emma, a marketing manager, noticed that the atmosphere was less formal than usual. She shifted from her typical business-focused discussions to sharing personal anecdotes and engaging in light-hearted banter. This adjustment helped her connect more easily with colleagues and foster a sense of camaraderie.

Reading the energy of the room and blending in seamlessly requires acute awareness of the social dynamics around you. Pay attention to the mood, body language, and conversational tone of the people you're with. For example, at a lively party, if the group is energetic and animated, joining in with enthusiasm and humor can help you fit in. Conversely, in a quieter, more introspective setting, adopting a more subdued and reflective approach can be more appropriate. Sarah, a consultant, excelled at this by carefully observing her surroundings and adjusting her behavior accordingly, making her interactions smooth and natural.

Building Rapport with Anyone

Building rapport is a fundamental aspect of social interactions, and it starts with finding common ground and demonstrating empathy.

Finding common ground with people from all walks of life is about identifying shared interests or experiences. This doesn't necessarily mean discussing hobbies or backgrounds; it can also involve finding mutual values or goals. For instance, during a business conference, Mark, a financial advisor, struck up a conversation with a fellow attendee about the challenges of balancing work and personal life. Despite their different professional backgrounds, they discovered a shared concern for work-life balance, which paved the way for a meaningful and engaging conversation.

The power of empathy in building instant rapport cannot be underestimated. Empathy involves understanding and sharing the feelings of others. When you show genuine interest in someone's experiences and emotions, it creates a connection that fosters trust and rapport. For example, when Lisa, a social worker, met a new client, she actively listened to their concerns and validated their feelings. Her empathetic approach helped establish a strong rapport, making the client feel understood and supported.

How to connect with different personality types effortlessly involves adapting your communication style to match the preferences of others. Some people are more analytical and appreciate detailed information, while others are more intuitive and value big-picture discussions. For example, when Tom, a project manager, interacted with a detail-oriented client, he provided thorough explanations and data to support his proposals. In contrast, when working with a visionary client, Tom focused on overarching goals and potential impacts. This flexibility allowed him to connect effectively with diverse personality types.

Leaving a Lasting Impression

Leaving a lasting impression involves not just the content of your conversation but also how you wrap it up and maintain the connection.

How to wrap up conversations in a memorable way is about leaving a positive and lasting note. Summarize key points of the conversation, express appreciation for the interaction, and offer a clear next step. For instance, if you've had a productive meeting with a potential client, you might say, "I've really enjoyed discussing your vision for the project. I'll send over a detailed proposal by Friday, and let's schedule a follow-up call next week." This approach ensures that the conversation ends on a high note and sets the stage for future interactions.

Creating an air of intrigue and leaving people wanting more involves engaging in conversations that pique interest and spark curiosity. Share interesting insights or stories without revealing everything, leaving your conversation partner eager to learn more. For example, during a social event, if you discuss an upcoming project you're excited about but keep the details vague, you might spark curiosity and anticipation. This intrigue can lead to further conversations and opportunities.

Maintaining connections after the initial meeting requires follow-up and ongoing engagement. Send a follow-up email or message expressing your enjoyment of the conversation and suggesting ways to stay in touch. For example, after meeting someone at a networking event, you might follow up with a LinkedIn connection request and a brief message, such as, "It was great meeting you at the event last week. I'd love to continue our conversation about [topic] and explore potential collaborations." This follow-up helps solidify the connection and demonstrates your genuine interest in maintaining the relationship.

Becoming a social chameleon involves more than just adapting to different environments; it requires mastering the art of rapport-building, leaving memorable impressions, and maintaining connections. By adjusting your approach to fit various social settings, connecting with diverse personalities, and ensuring that interactions end on a positive and engaging note, you can navigate any social situation with ease and make every interaction count. This adaptability not only enhances your social charm but also opens doors to meaningful connections and opportunities.

Chapter 4: The Art of Persuasion – Influencing People Without Being Pushy

Section 1: The Psychology of Persuasion

Persuasion is an essential skill in both personal and professional life, but it's often misunderstood as manipulation. True persuasion, however, is about understanding people's motivations and guiding them toward decisions that benefit everyone involved. When done right, it feels effortless, creating win-win situations that foster trust and respect. In this section, we'll explore the psychology of persuasion—why it works, how to use it ethically, and how subtle techniques can make a powerful impact without crossing the line into pushiness.

The Principles of Influence

At the heart of persuasion are universal principles that guide human behavior. Psychologist Dr. Robert Cialdini outlined six key principles of influence, three of which—reciprocity, scarcity, and authority—are particularly powerful in shaping how people respond to persuasive efforts.

How reciprocity, scarcity, and authority shape behavior begins with reciprocity, the idea that people are more likely to respond favorably when they feel they've been given something. This principle works because humans have a natural desire to return favors and maintain social equity. For instance, imagine you're at a networking event, and someone buys you a coffee or gives you helpful advice. You're more likely to feel inclined to offer something in return, whether it's future collaboration or a recommendation.

Scarcity is another powerful influencer. When something is perceived as rare or in limited supply, people are more likely to want it. In marketing, phrases like "limited time offer" or "only a few items left" tap into this instinct. But in personal interactions, you can use scarcity more subtly. For example, if you're leading a project and convey that your time or expertise is limited, others may value your input more and become more eager to work with you. It's not about being unavailable to manipulate interest but about framing your contributions as valuable.

Authority, the third principle, is about establishing credibility. People are more likely to be persuaded by someone who seems knowledgeable or experienced in a subject. For instance, if you've spent years mastering a particular skill, sharing that expertise in a conversation gives your opinions more weight. This doesn't mean you need to be boastful; rather, confidence and knowledge will speak for themselves, naturally boosting your persuasive power.

Building trust as the foundation for influence is essential. Trust is the bedrock on which all effective persuasion rests. Consider someone you trust implicitly—perhaps a mentor or close friend. When they offer advice or suggestions, you're more likely to follow them because you know they have your best interests at heart. In contrast, someone who lacks credibility or integrity will struggle to persuade, no matter how strong their argument is. Building trust requires consistency, honesty, and a genuine concern for others' well-being.

Understanding emotional triggers to persuade effectively is about tapping into the emotions that drive decision-making. Humans are emotional beings, and most of our decisions, even seemingly rational ones, are influenced by our feelings. For example, if you're trying to convince someone to support a cause, appealing to their empathy for the people affected is far more persuasive than presenting dry facts or statistics. When you understand what emotionally motivates someone—whether it's a desire for security, recognition, or belonging—you can frame your message in a way that resonates on a deeper level.

Subtle Persuasion Techniques

While some people believe persuasion requires bold, direct tactics, subtlety is often more effective. People generally resist feeling coerced or manipulated, so the art of persuasion involves guiding others to come to conclusions on their own.

How to suggest rather than demand is a key skill in this. Imagine you're a manager trying to get your team on board with a new strategy. Rather than issuing orders, you might present the benefits of the new approach and ask for their input. This invites collaboration and gives your team a sense of ownership over the decision, making them more likely to commit to the new plan. Subtle suggestions, phrased as questions or presented as options, allow people to feel like they're choosing to act rather than being forced.For example, I once worked with a colleague named Paul, who was highly effective at persuading others without them even realizing it. When he wanted someone to adopt a particular approach, he would phrase it as, "Have you considered trying it this way?" instead of saying, "You should do it this way." By framing his suggestion as a question, Paul invited others to think critically and often, they would come to the conclusion that his idea was the best option—making it feel like their own.

Using body language and tone of voice to persuade is another subtle yet powerful tool. Nonverbal cues, such as maintaining eye contact, nodding, and mirroring someone's posture, signal agreement and build rapport. Tone of voice plays a crucial role as well; a calm, steady tone conveys confidence and sincerity, making it easier to persuade others. In contrast, an aggressive or impatient tone can shut people down, even if your message is valid.

I once observed this in action during a negotiation between two business partners. One partner, Julia, remained calm and composed throughout the conversation, using a gentle but firm tone, while the other partner grew agitated. Julia's calm demeanor not only helped defuse the tension but also made her arguments more persuasive, leading the other partner to eventually agree with her points.

The power of gentle nudging vs. overt manipulation lies in the fact that people resist being manipulated, but they respond well to gentle encouragement. Nudging involves making small, subtle changes that influence decisions without taking away autonomy. For example, a restaurant might list its healthiest options first on the menu, gently nudging diners to choose those dishes without explicitly telling them what to order. Similarly, in personal relationships, you might subtly steer someone toward a particular decision by emphasizing the benefits of that choice rather than pushing them directly.

Appealing to People's Needs

At its core, effective persuasion is about aligning your goals with the needs and desires of others. When you can identify what someone truly wants, you can frame your message in a way that appeals to their self-interest.

Identifying the desires and pain points of others begins with listening and observing. People are constantly communicating their needs, whether verbally or through their actions. For example, in a sales situation, a customer might express concern about the durability of a product. If you understand that their underlying need is for reliability and long-term value, you can tailor your pitch to highlight those aspects of your offering.Once you've identified someone's desires, **speaking to their self-interest to align your goals** becomes much easier. Imagine you're trying to convince a colleague to take on a challenging project. Rather than focusing on why you need their help, frame the opportunity in terms of their career growth. Highlight how the project will allow them to showcase their skills and gain visibility within the company. By appealing to their self-interest, you make it easier for them to see how your request benefits them as well.

However, persuasion should never come across as insincere. **Using flattery without sounding disingenuous** is an art in itself. The key to making compliments work in your favor is to be specific and genuine. Instead of offering vague praise like, "You're really good at your job," which might come off as flattery, say something more thoughtful like, "I've noticed how you always handle client feedback with such grace—it's really impressive." This kind of specific recognition feels sincere and builds goodwill.

Persuasion is a nuanced art that involves understanding psychological principles, using subtle techniques, and appealing to the needs of others. When done correctly, it doesn't feel pushy or manipulative—it feels natural. By building trust, tapping into emotional triggers, and aligning your goals with the desires of others, you can influence people effectively while maintaining your integrity and charm. The true power of persuasion lies in its ability to create positive outcomes for both parties, making the process feel collaborative rather than coercive.

Chapter 4: The Art of Persuasion – Influencing People Without Being Pushy

Section 2: Persuading in Professional Settings

Persuasion in a professional setting requires a blend of tact, confidence, and finesse. Whether you're trying to win over clients, colleagues, or bosses, effective persuasion is more than just pushing your agenda. It's about understanding the needs and desires of those you're working with and aligning your goals with theirs. In this section, we'll explore the subtleties of persuasion in business environments, focusing on how to build rapport, create win-win outcomes, and present yourself and your ideas in a way that leaves a lasting impact.

Winning Over Clients or Colleagues

In any professional environment, your ability to build trust and rapport quickly can make or break deals and relationships. Whether you're working with a new client or trying to influence a colleague to support your vision, the foundation of persuasion is trust.

One of the most important lessons I learned early in my career was how quickly trust can be built—or eroded. I recall working on a major project with a client who was initially skeptical of my team's approach. Rather than pushing our agenda, we began by genuinely listening to their concerns and goals. We asked open-ended questions, allowing them to express their doubts freely. By acknowledging their concerns and incorporating their feedback into our proposal, we didn't just address their needs—we demonstrated that we were collaborators, not adversaries.

This approach—**building trust and rapport quickly in business**—relies on showing genuine interest in the other party's needs. By understanding their motivations, you can tailor your approach to fit their goals. The more you make it clear that your success is tied to theirs, the easier it becomes to persuade them. In the case of the client, we built such a strong relationship that, by the end of the project, they were advocating for our services to other departments within their company. We had successfully created a situation where both parties felt like winners.

Negotiation techniques that create win-win outcomes follow a similar principle. When negotiating in any professional setting, it's crucial to find common ground where both sides feel satisfied. This doesn't mean caving to every demand; it means framing your proposals in a way that addresses the other party's needs while meeting your own. For example, if you're negotiating a salary increase, instead of focusing solely on why you deserve more money, frame the conversation in terms of how your increased responsibilities or contributions are helping the company succeed. This way, you create a situation where both parties feel like they're gaining something valuable.

However, navigating office politics can be trickier, and **navigating office politics with charm and tact** is essential for long-term success. Office politics is often less about what you do and more about how you do it. Understanding the power dynamics and key players within your organization allows you to be strategic without being manipulative. For instance, when you align your goals with those of influential colleagues or superiors, you're not just pushing your own agenda—you're building alliances that will help you in the long run.

One of the most valuable strategies I've found is the art of subtle alignment. By identifying the goals of decision-makers and finding ways to support their initiatives, you become an asset in their eyes. This doesn't mean abandoning your principles or becoming overly compliant, but rather positioning yourself as someone who adds value to their objectives. Over time, this alignment creates influence without overtly seeking it.

The Elevator Pitch: Selling Yourself

Being able to distill your value into a short, impactful statement—**an elevator pitch**—is a critical skill in professional settings. The idea behind the elevator pitch is simple: Imagine you find yourself in an elevator with a decision-maker, and you only have 60 seconds to make an impression. What would you say?

Creating a concise, compelling pitch is about more than just reciting a rehearsed script; it's about making an emotional connection. Let's say you're pitching yourself for a promotion. Rather than listing your achievements, you might start with a story that illustrates how you solved a critical problem for the company. People remember stories more than they remember facts and figures. Your pitch should be designed to evoke emotion while showcasing your unique skills.

One of my favorite examples of an effective elevator pitch came from a colleague who was transitioning from a technical role to a leadership position. In her pitch, she didn't just highlight her technical expertise—she framed her experience in terms of how she had mentored junior employees and helped them grow, tying her personal value to the success of others. This not only made her memorable but also demonstrated that she was thinking beyond her immediate responsibilities.

Highlighting your value in 60 seconds or less can be daunting, but the key is to focus on what makes you different and why it matters. Ask yourself: What problems can you solve? What unique perspective do you bring? Tailor your pitch to highlight these points while keeping the listener's needs in mind. If you're speaking to a potential client, for example, focus on how your skills or services will solve their specific challenges.

Tailoring your message to different audiences is equally important. A pitch that works for a client might not work for your boss or a colleague. Different audiences care about different things, so adjust your message accordingly. For a client, focus on results and benefits. For a boss, emphasize how your contributions support the broader company goals. By understanding your audience's priorities, you can craft a message that resonates with them on a deeper level.

Presenting Your Ideas with Impact

When it comes to influencing others in a professional setting, how you present your ideas is just as important as the ideas themselves. Whether you're leading a meeting, delivering a presentation, or simply sharing your thoughts in a brainstorming session, **presenting your ideas with impact** requires a blend of confidence, clarity, and persuasion.

One of the most effective ways to do this is through storytelling. **Engaging your audience with storytelling and data** creates an emotional connection, making your message more memorable. For example, if you're pitching a new project to your team, rather than diving straight into the technical details, you could start by painting a picture of the problem you're trying to solve. Walk your audience through the real-world impact of the issue, then transition into how your solution addresses it. This approach not only captures attention but also helps your audience see the bigger picture.

Data is equally important, especially in professional settings where decisions are often made based on measurable outcomes. But data alone can be dry, so it's essential to weave it into a narrative. For instance, if you're presenting sales data, don't just throw out numbers—explain what those numbers mean in terms of future growth opportunities or potential risks. When you combine facts with stories, you create a persuasive argument that appeals to both logic and emotion.

Of course, not every idea will be met with immediate approval. **Addressing objections calmly and confidently** is a crucial part of the persuasion process. When someone challenges your ideas, resist the urge to become defensive. Instead, acknowledge their concerns and use them as an opportunity to strengthen your case. For example, if a colleague raises a potential flaw in your proposal, thank them for their input and explain how you've accounted for that risk. This not only demonstrates that you're open to feedback but also shows that you've thought through the potential challenges.

A few years ago, I was part of a team that was pitching a new software system to upper management. During the meeting, one of the executives raised concerns about the cost and implementation time. Rather than pushing back, we acknowledged their concerns and presented data showing how the system's long-term benefits—such as increased productivity and reduced maintenance costs—would outweigh the initial investment. By calmly addressing the objection and reinforcing our argument with data, we were able to win approval for the project.

In the world of business, persuasion isn't about forcing others to see things your way—it's about building trust, aligning your goals with theirs, and presenting your ideas in a way that resonates. Whether you're navigating office politics, crafting a powerful elevator pitch, or presenting your ideas in a meeting, the ability to persuade others without being pushy is an invaluable skill that can elevate your professional success.

Chapter 4: The Art of Persuasion – Influencing People Without Being Pushy

Section 3: Persuasion in Social and Romantic Scenarios

Persuasion in social and romantic settings is a delicate art. Unlike in professional environments, where logic and data often play key roles, the dynamics in personal relationships rely more on emotional intelligence, subtle cues, and a genuine interest in others. Whether you're trying to make a meaningful connection with someone you just met or integrate into a new social circle, the key is to influence without overwhelming, to engage without dominating. Let's explore how you can navigate these delicate situations with ease and charm.

Flirting Without Trying Too Hard

When it comes to romantic persuasion, one of the biggest mistakes people make is trying too hard. You've likely encountered situations where someone's desperation to impress comes off as awkward or off-putting. The key to successful flirting isn't about overcompensating or using scripted lines—it's about creating a comfortable, enjoyable atmosphere where both parties feel intrigued.

I remember a conversation I had with a friend, Jake, who always seemed to be the center of attention in social settings, especially with women. What set Jake apart wasn't that he was constantly flirting in the traditional sense; it was that he knew how to **show interest without appearing needy**. His secret? Confidence and curiosity. He asked genuine questions, actively listened, and responded in a way that made the other person feel heard. He never forced the conversation, and he never rushed to impress.

Instead of seeking validation or trying to "win" someone over, **reading romantic cues** became second nature to Jake. If the conversation naturally deepened, he would let it flow, adding subtle humor or a personal anecdote when appropriate. If he sensed hesitation or disengagement, he gracefully allowed the moment to pass, knowing that not every interaction needed to be a grand romantic gesture.

This approach makes romantic persuasion feel effortless. **Turning casual conversations into deeper connections** happens when you're comfortable with yourself and the other person. By maintaining a relaxed demeanor, you invite them to share more about themselves, building a sense of trust. The key is to balance intrigue with attentiveness, signaling that you're interested without appearing overbearing.

Winning Over New Social Circles

In social scenarios, especially when you're entering an established group, there's an unspoken challenge of balancing assertiveness with humility. Nobody wants to come across as the person trying to force their way into a circle, yet you also don't want to fade into the background.

I once had a colleague, Sarah, who effortlessly became part of any group she encountered. What was striking about Sarah's approach was her ability to **integrate smoothly into existing friend groups** without making waves. She observed first, understanding the group dynamics, and when she finally joined in, she contributed in ways that felt natural and unforced. She never tried to dominate conversations, but when she spoke, her insights were thoughtful and engaging. This allowed her to earn respect and admiration quickly.

In social settings, becoming the person people naturally gravitate toward requires a combination of empathy and confidence. You need to **balance confidence with humility**, showing that you're comfortable with who you are but also respectful of the existing dynamics. Sarah had an incredible knack for this. At a house party, for instance, she never bulldozed her way into conversations. Instead, she quietly listened, laughed when appropriate, and gradually offered her perspective when she felt the moment was right. By showing genuine interest in the people around her, she became a magnet for others, and soon enough, she was the one people sought out for conversation.

What made Sarah successful wasn't just her attentiveness—it was her ability to subtly shift the focus from herself to others. People love talking about themselves, and if you can **ask the right questions** while offering your thoughts in a balanced way, you'll find that social integration happens naturally. Sarah's humility wasn't about downplaying her accomplishments, but about understanding that relationships are built on shared experiences, not showmanship.

The Art of Convincing Without Dominating

In social and romantic persuasion, there's a fine line between leading a conversation and overwhelming it. Some people mistakenly think that to persuade others, they need to talk more, control the narrative, or showcase their intelligence. However, true persuasion often comes through subtlety—by making others feel like they've arrived at a decision on their own

Take, for instance, a time when I was at a dinner party where a heated debate about travel destinations was taking place. One guest, Marcus, held strong opinions about the best places to visit in Europe. Rather than overpowering the conversation with facts, he chose to **lead the conversation without overpowering others** by allowing room for different perspectives. He acknowledged opposing views and offered questions that invited others to expand on their ideas.

Marcus understood that **persuading through listening and understanding** was far more effective than simply dominating the conversation. As people shared their experiences, Marcus gently nudged them to consider alternative viewpoints—his viewpoints—but he never made anyone feel as if they were wrong. In the end, people were not only swayed by his suggestions but felt that the discussion had been inclusive and enriching. Marcus didn't need to force anyone to agree with him; they arrived there organically, thanks to his ability to listen and guide rather than dictate.

This approach works because it fosters **mutual respect and admiration**. By demonstrating that you're willing to hear others out, even if you ultimately have a differing opinion, you create an atmosphere where persuasion feels like collaboration, not competition. In romantic settings, this is equally important. If you're constantly trying to dominate the conversation, the other person will feel overwhelmed or undervalued. But if you allow the conversation to ebb and flow naturally, you build rapport, which lays the foundation for mutual attraction.

Finding the Balance in Persuasion

At the heart of persuasion in social and romantic scenarios is the art of balance. You want to lead without forcing, charm without trying too hard, and win others over without dominating. This balance comes down to self-awareness and empathy.

Being self-aware allows you to gauge your own energy and presence. Are you monopolizing the conversation? Are you subtly seeking validation, or are you genuinely interested in the person or group you're engaging with? It's about keeping your ego in check, knowing that true connection is built on reciprocity, not one-sided monologues.

Empathy, on the other hand, allows you to read the energy and needs of others. In social and romantic settings, people often communicate more through their body language and tone than their words. By tuning into these subtle signals, you can adjust your approach to meet the moment. If someone seems disengaged or uncomfortable, back off. If they're intrigued or excited, lean in.

The best persuaders aren't those who talk the loudest or the most—they're the ones who create space for others, who elevate the conversation by making people feel heard and valued. Whether you're flirting with someone you're interested in or trying to win over a new social group, the key is to make the interaction feel effortless. People will always gravitate toward those who make them feel good about themselves.

At the end of the day, social and romantic persuasion isn't about being manipulative—it's about creating genuine connections through understanding, attentiveness, and balance. The more you can master these subtle cues, the more effortlessly persuasive you'll become in all areas of your life.

Chapter 5: The Power of Emotional Intelligence – Reading People and Responding with Finesse

Section 1: Understanding Emotional Intelligence

In the world of charm, influence, and social success, few traits are as powerful as emotional intelligence (EQ). Emotional intelligence isn't just about being aware of emotions; it's about understanding them, managing them, and using that knowledge to build meaningful relationships. People often think that charisma is all about wit, looks, or confidence, but the truth is that **emotional intelligence** is at the core of being truly suave. Understanding your own emotions and the emotions of those around you can transform the way you interact with others, enhancing your personal and professional life.

What Emotional Intelligence (EQ) Is

At its most basic, **emotional intelligence** is the ability to recognize and understand your emotions and the emotions of others, and to use that awareness to manage interactions effectively. Think about it as the skill to read the room, to know when to speak, when to listen, and how to react with empathy and tact. It's not something you can fake; genuine emotional intelligence shines through in every conversation, interaction, and connection.

A suave man with high emotional intelligence knows that **self-awareness** is key. Being able to recognize your emotional state is the first step toward controlling it. Imagine you're about to walk into an important meeting, and you feel a wave of anxiety wash over you. A man with high EQ will notice that anxiety, take a moment to calm himself, and walk in with composure, projecting confidence.

A friend of mine, Daniel, demonstrated this effortlessly when we worked on a group project together. Everyone was under intense pressure, and the stakes were high. While most of us were on edge, snapping at each other over minor disagreements, Daniel remained calm. He wasn't without emotion—he admitted feeling the pressure—but he never let it dictate his actions. Instead, he focused on solutions and helped others do the same. His emotional awareness gave him a level-headedness that made people want to follow his lead.

Emotional intelligence is not just about managing your own emotions, though. It's about understanding the emotions of others. Whether it's recognizing when someone is uncomfortable, identifying when someone needs encouragement, or knowing how to navigate complex emotional landscapes, this ability makes you not only charming but also deeply relatable.

The 5 Pillars of Emotional Intelligence

The foundation of emotional intelligence can be broken down into five key components: **self-awareness**, **self-regulation**, **motivation**, **empathy**, and **social skills**. Each of these plays a crucial role in developing a sophisticated emotional intelligence that helps you thrive in all areas of life.

1. Self-awareness

Self-awareness is the cornerstone of emotional intelligence. It's the ability to recognize your feelings as they happen and understand how they affect your thoughts and behavior. This awareness allows you to make conscious choices in every situation. A suave man doesn't react impulsively; he pauses, assesses, and decides how to proceed.

I once watched my colleague, James, a man with incredible self-awareness, handle a tense negotiation. As the conversation grew more heated, I could see his frustration building, but instead of lashing out, he paused, took a breath, and chose his words carefully. His ability to regulate his emotions on the spot changed the entire dynamic, turning a potential conflict into a productive discussion.

2. Self-regulation

Self-regulation is about controlling your emotions and impulses—especially in difficult situations. It's the ability to stay calm under pressure, avoid hasty decisions, and remain composed even when things don't go your way. This isn't about suppressing emotions but about managing them effectively.

A suave man, like James in the negotiation, uses **self-regulation** to prevent outbursts or rash decisions. In social settings, this could mean resisting the urge to say something sarcastic when you're irritated, or keeping your cool when someone else is upset. It's about being steady, someone others can rely on to stay calm no matter what.

3. Motivation

Motivation in the context of emotional intelligence refers to having a passion for achieving your goals and inspiring others to do the same. It's not just about external rewards; it's about an internal drive to improve, to strive for excellence. Suave men are often highly motivated, but they don't flaunt it; their drive is quiet but powerful.

Consider Steve, a close friend of mine, who has this inner drive. His quiet but unshakeable confidence comes from knowing that he's working toward his own goals, and that sense of purpose influences everything he does. He doesn't boast about his achievements, but you can sense his commitment and motivation just by being around him. People are drawn to his energy because it's genuine, not flashy.

4. Empathy

Empathy might be one of the most important skills in any social interaction. It's the ability to understand what others are feeling and respond in a way that makes them feel seen and heard. For a suave man, **empathy** is the secret weapon that builds strong, lasting connections.

I once witnessed a powerful example of empathy in action at a social event. My friend Alex, who has an uncanny ability to connect with people, noticed a newcomer standing awkwardly at the edge of the crowd. Without making a big deal of it, he walked over, started a conversation, and soon had the person feeling completely at ease. By recognizing and responding to the other person's discomfort, Alex demonstrated emotional intelligence, making a memorable impression without effort.

Empathy is not just about comforting others in moments of distress. It's about understanding what drives people, what they care about, and how you can engage with them in a way that matters. When you can connect with someone on that deeper emotional level, your charisma becomes undeniable.

5. Social Skills

Finally, social skills are the ability to manage relationships, build networks, and maintain connections. High emotional intelligence means you know how to communicate effectively, resolve conflicts, and inspire others. Social skills are not just about being friendly; they're about being influential in a way that people trust and admire.

One of my mentors, Mike, was a master at this. He could walk into any room and within minutes, people gravitated toward him. It wasn't just his charm—it was his genuine interest in others and his ability to make them feel important. He was a natural networker, but he never came across as self-serving. His social skills were rooted in emotional intelligence, and that's what made him magnetic.

Why Suave Men Excel in Emotional Intelligence

What makes suave men particularly successful in life is their ability to **excel in emotional intelligence**. Whether in personal relationships or professional settings, emotional intelligence sets them apart because it allows them to navigate complex social dynamics with ease and charm.

One of the most striking traits of emotionally intelligent men is their **emotional control**. They don't let their emotions dictate their behavior, but they also don't hide them. Instead, they use their emotional awareness to enhance their charisma. For example, in moments of stress or tension, they project calm, which in turn makes others feel safe and confident in their presence.

Empathy, too, plays a critical role in their charm. **Empathy is the secret to lasting connections** because it shows others that you care about their feelings, that you're not just in it for yourself. Think of suave men like Barack Obama or Will Smith, who seem to have an innate ability to connect with people from all walks of life. What sets them apart isn't just their talent or success—it's their emotional intelligence, their ability to read the room, understand others, and respond in ways that build trust and connection.

In every social interaction, emotional intelligence gives suave men the upper hand. They aren't just reacting to the moment—they're guiding it, using their self-awareness, empathy, and social skills to influence the outcome. Whether it's diffusing a heated argument, making someone feel valued, or motivating a team to success, emotional intelligence is the key to mastering the art of persuasion and charm. And in a world where relationships are everything, it's this emotional finesse that truly sets suave men apart.

Chapter 5: The Power of Emotional Intelligence – Reading People and Responding with Finesse

Section 2: Reading and Responding to Social Cues

Mastering the art of emotional intelligence doesn't stop at understanding your own emotions. It's equally important to be able to read the emotions of those around you. The ability to pick up on subtle social cues—whether it's body language, tone of voice, or facial expressions—can elevate your interactions and make you not only more persuasive but also more likable. By understanding these cues and adjusting your behavior accordingly, you can create emotional resonance with others, making them feel seen, heard, and valued.

Identifying Emotional Signals

When it comes to reading people, body language often speaks louder than words. The way someone stands, the movement of their eyes, or a subtle shift in their posture can give you critical information about how they're feeling. It's almost like learning a second language—once you know how to interpret these signals, you can navigate any social interaction with ease.For example, let's say you're at a networking event and you've been talking to someone for a few minutes. You notice that they've started to glance around the room more frequently or take small steps backward. These are classic signs of disengagement. They're probably looking for an exit from the conversation but don't want to seem rude. Recognizing this early on allows you to shift the energy of the conversation or wrap it up gracefully.

One evening at a dinner party, I observed a friend, Laura, who was excellent at reading these kinds of social cues. She was engaged in a conversation with a mutual acquaintance who seemed initially interested, but as the night wore on, his body language shifted—he crossed his arms, leaned back in his chair, and started looking around the room. Laura quickly recognized these signals and smoothly transitioned the conversation to a lighter topic before eventually excusing herself. Rather than letting the conversation fizzle out awkwardly, she left on a high note, preserving the connection and leaving the other person with a positive impression.

Facial expressions are another goldmine of emotional information. A person's smile can tell you whether they're genuinely interested or merely being polite. A furrowed brow might indicate confusion or discomfort, while widened eyes can signify excitement or surprise. Being able to interpret these small changes can give you valuable insights into how the other person is feeling in real time, allowing you to adjust your approach accordingly.

Tone of voice is equally important. The same sentence can have entirely different meanings depending on how it's delivered. A flat, monotone delivery might signal boredom or disinterest, while a warm, energetic tone can show enthusiasm. If you're discussing a serious topic and notice that the other person's tone shifts to a higher pitch or becomes softer, it could indicate discomfort or emotional vulnerability. Recognizing these shifts in tone helps you gauge whether you should proceed, shift the conversation, or offer reassurance.

Adapting Your Approach Based on Cues

Once you've identified the emotional signals others are sending, the next step is to adapt your approach accordingly. A conversation that starts out smoothly can quickly derail if you miss the subtle cues indicating a change in the other person's emotional state. By being flexible and responsive, you can keep the conversation flowing in a positive direction.

For instance, if you're discussing a topic and notice that the other person becomes fidgety or their smile starts to fade, it might be a sign that they're uncomfortable. This could be due to the subject matter or even something as simple as fatigue. A suave individual knows how to read the room and shift gears, perhaps by asking a lighter question or changing the subject entirely. By doing so, you keep the conversation balanced and avoid making the other person feel trapped or uneasy.

I once witnessed a masterful example of this during a company meeting. The speaker was going into great detail about a new project when he noticed that the team members were starting to glance at their watches and shift in their seats—subtle signs that they were losing interest. Rather than plowing through his presentation, he paused, cracked a light joke, and then pivoted to a more engaging, interactive discussion. By adjusting his approach based on the social cues in the room, he kept everyone engaged and avoided a disconnect.

When you're able to **adjust your communication style** based on others' emotional states, you create a much more harmonious and fluid interaction. You might, for example, tone down an enthusiastic pitch if you notice someone is feeling overwhelmed, or step up your energy if the conversation is starting to drag. Understanding the art of give-and-take is key to maintaining rapport.

Finally, knowing **when to exit a conversation gracefully** is just as important as knowing how to start one. If you sense that the other person is growing restless or distracted, don't force the interaction to continue. Instead, look for a natural opportunity to wrap up the conversation on a high note. A simple, "It was great chatting with you. I'll let you get back to the event, but let's connect again soon," shows that you're attuned to their feelings and respectful of their time.

Creating Emotional Resonance

Emotional resonance is the feeling you get when someone truly "gets" you—when they mirror your emotions and make you feel understood. This is the secret sauce to building deep, meaningful connections, and it's something emotionally intelligent individuals excel at. **Mirroring emotions** is a powerful tool for creating rapport because it signals to the other person that you're on the same page, emotionally speaking.

One of the simplest ways to create emotional resonance is through body language. When someone leans in to speak to you, lean in slightly as well. When they smile, return the smile. This isn't about mimicking every gesture they make, but about subtly aligning your energy with theirs to build a sense of mutual understanding. Research shows that people tend to like others who mirror their body language, as it creates an unconscious bond.

Take my friend Mark, for example. At a social gathering, he always seems to click with everyone he meets. He does this by not only listening to what people say but also mirroring their emotions. If someone's excited, he matches that energy. If they're upset, he tones down his responses and shows genuine empathy. People walk away from conversations with Mark feeling heard, valued, and understood.

Empathy is another critical component of emotional resonance. To truly connect with someone, you have to be able to step into their shoes and understand their feelings. This doesn't mean you have to agree with them, but simply acknowledging their emotions can go a long way in building rapport. If a colleague is frustrated about a project, saying something like, "I can see how that would be really stressful," lets them know you're attuned to their emotions, which fosters trust.

Creating emotional resonance also means making people feel **understood and valued**. This involves active listening—focusing not only on what someone is saying but also on what they're feeling. Pay attention to the emotion behind their words, and respond in a way that acknowledges those feelings. If a friend is venting about a tough day, instead of jumping in with advice, try reflecting their emotions back to them: "That sounds like a really difficult situation. I'd be feeling frustrated too." Simple, empathetic responses like this show that you're not just hearing the words—they make the other person feel emotionally supported.

Lastly, to create a lasting impression, leave people with a positive emotional takeaway. Whether it's by sharing a lighthearted comment at the end of a serious conversation or offering encouragement, your ability to make others feel good after the interaction is what sets the suave man apart. Emotional resonance lingers long after the conversation has ended, solidifying your place in their memory as someone who truly connects on a deeper level.

In summary, reading and responding to social cues is an essential skill for anyone who wants to excel in personal and professional interactions. By paying attention to body language, facial expressions, and tone of voice, you can adjust your approach in real-time to maintain rapport and build trust. Creating emotional resonance through empathy and emotional mirroring makes others feel understood and valued, deepening the connection and leaving a lasting impression. When you master these skills, you not only enhance your social charm but also unlock the power to influence and connect with people on a meaningful level.

Chapter 5: The Power of Emotional Intelligence – Reading People and Responding with Finesse

Section 3: Handling Conflict with Charm and Diplomacy

Conflict is an inevitable part of life, whether it arises in personal relationships, the workplace, or casual social interactions. While many people view conflict as something to avoid, the emotionally intelligent man sees it as an opportunity for growth, connection, and even persuasion. When handled with charm and diplomacy, conflict can actually strengthen relationships and leave lasting positive impressions.

Mastering the art of handling conflict requires understanding its roots, defusing tension with finesse, and turning disagreements into opportunities for collaboration and connection.

Recognizing the Roots of Conflict

The first step in handling any conflict is to recognize where it stems from. Often, disagreements are not purely about the issue at hand, but rather about underlying emotional triggers. People bring their past experiences, insecurities, and frustrations into interactions, and these unspoken emotions can fuel conflicts more than the surface-level problem.For instance, imagine you're having a disagreement with a colleague about how to approach a project. The conflict might seem like it's about a difference in strategy, but beneath the surface, your colleague might be feeling undervalued, stressed, or threatened. If you respond only to the argument about strategy without acknowledging the emotional undercurrent, the conflict is likely to escalate.

In a situation like this, emotionally intelligent individuals know how to pause and ask themselves, "What is this person really feeling?" By putting yourself in their shoes and considering what unspoken emotions might be driving their behavior, you can respond with empathy instead of reacting impulsively. This simple shift in perspective can dramatically change the course of the conversation.

One example of how unrecognized emotional triggers can escalate a situation occurred during a group project I worked on in college. A teammate, Sarah, was particularly harsh in rejecting my ideas, which initially annoyed me. I could have reacted defensively, but instead, I took a step back and realized she was under a lot of pressure due to personal issues. By acknowledging her stress in a subtle, empathetic way, I was able to steer the conversation toward collaboration rather than confrontation. This not only diffuses the tension but also strengthens our working relationship.

Unresolved emotions are often the silent force that turns minor disagreements into major disputes. When someone feels unheard or disrespected, their frustration can build over time, making even small conflicts seem overwhelming. This is why it's important to address conflicts early, with an emphasis on understanding the other person's perspective rather than jumping to conclusions or assuming the worst.

Defusing Tension with Charm

Once you've recognized the emotional roots of a conflict, the next step is to **defuse the tension** in a way that's both calming and respectful. One of the most powerful tools in this process is maintaining your composure. Staying calm when others are agitated allows you to guide the conversation in a productive direction, setting the tone for a more respectful exchange. The key to staying calm lies in emotional regulation. Instead of reacting with anger or frustration when tensions rise, the suave man knows how to breathe, center himself, and respond thoughtfully. This doesn't mean suppressing your emotions; it means managing them in a way that supports constructive dialogue.

Another effective technique for diffusing conflict is to use **humor** and lightness. Humor, when used appropriately, can break the tension and remind both parties that the situation isn't as dire as it seems. It's important, though, to use humor tactfully. It should never come across as dismissive or condescending. Rather, it should serve to lighten the mood, showing that you're not taking the conflict personally and that you're willing to find common ground.

For example, a friend of mine, Jake, has a natural ability to de-escalate conflicts by inserting a lighthearted comment at just the right moment. During a heated debate with a group of friends about politics, the conversation was on the verge of getting ugly. Jake, sensing the rising tension, smiled and quipped, "Well, at least we can all agree that pizza is the ultimate bipartisan meal." It was a simple joke, but it shifted the energy of the conversation, diffused the tension, and allowed everyone to take a step back and regain perspective.

Active listening is another crucial skill in conflict resolution. Often, people in a conflict just want to be heard. By truly listening to the other person's grievances—without interrupting or planning your rebuttal while they're speaking—you demonstrate respect and empathy. Active listening involves nodding, maintaining eye contact, and occasionally summarizing what the other person has said to show that you're paying attention. This not only helps to calm the other person but also allows you to fully understand their perspective, which is key to resolving the conflict.

For example, during a disagreement with a friend about a shared decision, I made a point of listening to her frustrations without interrupting. I then reflected her concerns back to her by saying, "I can see how this decision has made you feel overlooked, and that wasn't my intention." That simple act of acknowledging her feelings changed the entire tone of the conversation. We were able to move from arguing to working together to find a solution that worked for both of us.

Turning Conflict into Opportunity

Finally, a master of emotional intelligence doesn't just stop at defusing conflict; they know how to turn it into an **opportunity for growth** and stronger connections. This starts with finding **common ground**. Most conflicts are not a result of fundamentally opposing values but rather a misunderstanding of priorities. By focusing on what you agree on rather than what you disagree on, you can shift the conversation from blame to collaboration.

For instance, in a professional setting, if you're in a heated negotiation, find areas where both parties share a common goal. By focusing on shared interests, you create a foundation for resolving the conflict in a way that benefits both sides.

I recall a situation where a colleague and I were in disagreement about a project timeline. Instead of continuing to argue, we both realized that we were ultimately working toward the same goal: delivering a high-quality product. Once we acknowledged that common goal, the conversation shifted from blame to problem-solving. We worked together to find a compromise on the timeline that satisfied both of us, and the project ultimately benefited from our collaborative approach.

Diplomacy is key in turning conflicts into opportunities. This means maintaining respect for the other person's perspective while still standing your ground. Diplomacy is about guiding the conversation toward solutions rather than getting bogged down in the details of the disagreement. For example, rather than saying, "You're wrong," say, "I see your point, but here's another perspective we should consider." This phrasing keeps the conversation respectful and solution-focused while ensuring your viewpoint is heard.

In romantic or social situations, conflicts can be even more emotionally charged. The ability to remain diplomatic, yet emotionally attuned, is essential in these cases. For instance, during a disagreement with a partner, rather than reacting defensively, you can say, "I understand how you're feeling, and I don't want us to argue. Let's figure out how we can both feel better about this situation." By focusing on solutions instead of escalating emotions, you turn the conflict into an opportunity for deeper connection.

Conclusion

Handling conflict with charm and diplomacy is a hallmark of high emotional intelligence. By recognizing the emotional triggers that fuel conflict, staying calm under pressure, and actively listening, you can defuse tension and guide conversations toward productive outcomes. More importantly, the emotionally intelligent man views conflict as an opportunity for growth and stronger connections, using diplomacy to maintain respect while finding common ground.

In any social or professional setting, conflict doesn't have to be a negative experience. When approached with empathy, humor, and tact, disagreements can lead to more meaningful relationships, improved collaboration, and a deeper understanding of others. Through emotional intelligence, conflict becomes less about winning or losing and more about fostering connection and resolution—proving that even in moments of tension, the suave man remains composed, charming, and influential.

Chapter 6: Body Language Mastery – Speaking Volumes Without Saying a Word

Section 1: The Science of Nonverbal Communication

Body language is one of the most powerful forms of communication, and it often speaks louder than words. Whether you're conscious of it or not, the way you stand, sit, move, or make eye contact sends strong signals to those around you. For suave men who want to master the art of charm and persuasion, understanding the science of nonverbal communication is essential.

Why Body Language Is More Important Than Words

Research suggests that 70-90% of communication is nonverbal, meaning that what you say is often less important than how you say it. Think of a time when someone told you they were "fine," but their body language told you a completely different story. Their arms might have been crossed, their posture stiff, and their eye contact minimal. You didn't believe their words because their nonverbal cues revealed their true feelings.

Nonverbal communication operates largely at a subconscious level. People often pick up on cues without even realizing it, and they form judgments based on those cues before you've had a chance to say much at all. For example, a handshake that is too weak might signal lack of confidence or enthusiasm, while one that is too firm can come across as aggressive. These subtle interactions set the tone for how others perceive you.

In social and professional settings, people make rapid judgments about your trustworthiness, competence, and authority based on your body language. This is why a man who masters nonverbal cues can navigate conversations and interactions with ease, even when he says very little. The suave man understands that how he presents himself physically is critical to his overall charm and influence.

Take, for instance, the way politicians and public speakers command a room without saying a word. Their posture is upright, their gestures are deliberate, and their eye contact makes each person in the audience feel engaged. These individuals understand that words alone cannot carry their message. The way they use their bodies amplifies their credibility and impact.

The Key Elements of Body Language

Eye Contact

One of the most important elements of body language is **eye contact**. When used correctly, it builds trust, conveys confidence, and creates a sense of connection. Conversely, avoiding eye contact can make you appear unsure, distracted, or even dishonest. The key to mastering eye contact is balance—you don't want to stare someone down, but you also don't want to glance away too often. A good rule of thumb is to maintain eye contact for about 60-70% of the conversation. This shows that you're engaged and interested without coming off as overbearing.For example, during a job interview, maintaining eye contact with your interviewer signals that you are confident and focused. It helps to establish a rapport and makes your responses seem more sincere. In contrast, frequently looking away or down at your hands might give the impression that you're nervous or unsure of your qualifications.

Posture

Posture is another crucial component of body language. How you carry yourself speaks volumes about your level of self-assurance and how others should perceive you. Slouching or hunching over can signal a lack of confidence or energy, while standing tall with your shoulders back and chest open demonstrates authority and poise.

Think of how someone like Dwayne "The Rock" Johnson walks into a room. His posture commands attention and respect before he even speaks. This is the kind of presence suave men aim to project, whether in a business meeting or a social setting. A strong posture not only affects how others see you, but it also influences how you feel about yourself. Studies have shown that adopting a confident stance can boost your own feelings of power and reduce stress, making you more effective in social situations.

When sitting, avoid slumping or crossing your arms, which can make you seem closed off. Instead, sit with your back straight, hands resting comfortably, and feet planted firmly on the floor. This conveys openness and readiness to engage.

Gestures

Gestures are another way to emphasize your points and add weight to your words. However, it's important not to overdo it. Too many gestures can come across as erratic or overly emotional, while too few can make you seem rigid or disinterested. The key is to use your hands deliberately, to underscore important points in a way that feels natural.

For example, making open-handed gestures, like showing your palms, signals honesty and transparency. When people see your hands, they instinctively trust you more. On the other hand, hiding your hands in your pockets or behind your back can signal that you have something to hide.

Similarly, gestures that involve touching your face, like rubbing your chin or covering your mouth, can be interpreted as signs of nervousness or deception. By keeping your gestures purposeful and open, you reinforce the impression that you're confident, calm, and in control.

Understanding Cultural Differences in Body Language

One of the subtleties of body language is that it can vary significantly across cultures. What is considered confident or polite in one culture might be seen as aggressive or disrespectful in another. For the suave man who frequently finds himself in international or cross-cultural settings, understanding these differences is critical to avoiding misunderstandings and ensuring effective communication.

For instance, in many Western cultures, direct eye contact is a sign of confidence and attentiveness. However, in some Asian and Middle Eastern cultures, prolonged eye contact can be considered rude or confrontational. Similarly, personal space varies greatly from culture to culture. In the United States, people tend to prefer more personal space, while in many Latin

American and Mediterranean cultures, standing closer to one another is the norm and shows friendliness.

A great example of adapting body language to cultural differences can be seen in the way diplomats or international business people conduct themselves. They often take the time to learn about the customs of the people they will be interacting with, ensuring that their gestures and nonverbal communication don't unintentionally offend. When I traveled to Japan for a business trip, I noticed that bowing was an important part of greeting and showing respect. While handshakes were acceptable, incorporating a slight bow into my introduction went a long way in establishing rapport.

To be suave in cross-cultural settings, you need to be aware of these differences and adjust your nonverbal communication accordingly. This doesn't mean changing who you are, but it does mean being flexible and respectful of the norms of others.

Avoiding Common Body Language Mistakes

One of the most common mistakes people make when it comes to body language is crossing their arms during conversations. While this might feel comfortable, it often sends the message that you're defensive or closed off. A more open stance, with your arms relaxed by your sides or your hands resting on a table, creates a much more approachable and confident impression.

Another common mistake is failing to match your facial expressions with the emotions you're trying to convey. For example, if you're delivering exciting news but your face remains neutral, the mismatch can confuse your audience and lessen the impact of your message. Ensure that your expressions are in sync with your tone and words.

Touching your face or fidgeting with objects like pens or phones can also detract from your confidence and focus. These behaviors signal nervousness or distraction, making it harder for people to fully engage with what you're saying.

Conclusion

Mastering nonverbal communication is about much more than knowing the right gestures or maintaining good posture. It's about being aware of the messages your body is sending at all times, whether you're in a boardroom, on a date, or meeting someone for the first time. A man who can control his body language has a silent, but powerful, tool for influencing others and leaving a lasting impression.

From the confidence that comes with maintaining strong posture and eye contact, to the subtle art of reading and responding to others' body language cues, the science of nonverbal communication is essential for anyone looking to enhance their social skills. When you learn to speak volumes without saying a word, you become more persuasive, more trustworthy, and more effortlessly suave.

Understanding cultural differences and avoiding common mistakes will take you one step further toward true mastery of nonverbal communication. Whether you're meeting new people, navigating professional settings, or simply wanting to make a lasting impression, your body language will often be the first—and most impactful—message you send.

Chapter 6: Body Language Mastery – Speaking Volumes Without Saying a Word

Section 2: Projecting Confidence and Charisma with Body Language

Body language is not just about gestures or posture; it's about how you project confidence and charisma in any social setting. The way you stand, move, and engage with people can either make you seem like the most magnetic person in the room or someone who's easily overlooked. A suave man understands how to use body language to create a lasting impression and influence others without uttering a word.

The Power Pose

Before stepping into any important event—a meeting, a social gathering, or a presentation—it's crucial to prepare not just your words but also your body language. The concept of the **power pose** comes from research in psychology that suggests adopting confident body postures can actually change your mindset. When you take up space with open, expansive gestures, your brain responds by boosting feelings of confidence.

For example, imagine you're about to give a major presentation at work. You're standing outside the room, feeling the tension building. One trick many successful individuals use is to take a few minutes to adopt a power pose: standing tall with your feet planted firmly on the ground, your hands on your hips, shoulders back, and chest open. Holding this stance for two minutes can lower cortisol (the stress hormone) and increase testosterone (the hormone linked to dominance and confidence).

In fact, think of athletes before a big game—arms raised in victory even before the event starts. This open posture not only makes them feel empowered, but it also signals to others that they are in control. By using a power pose before stepping into a high-pressure situation, you can shift your internal state from anxious to assured. You'll walk in with a sense of authority, and your body language will reflect that.

The Impact of Open, Expansive Postures in Social Situations

Once you're in the room, maintaining **open, expansive postures** helps signal confidence and draws others toward you. Closed-off body language—crossed arms, hunched shoulders, or shrinking into yourself—sends a message that you're either disinterested or insecure. However, standing tall, keeping your arms relaxed by your side or using gestures that invite others into the conversation, communicates that you're self-assured and approachable.

Take, for instance, a networking event. You're surrounded by strangers, and your natural instinct might be to cross your arms as a protective measure or hide behind your phone. But to project charisma, it's essential to do the opposite. Instead, stand with your feet slightly apart, arms open, and shoulders relaxed.

Smile and make eye contact with those around you. This stance signals to others that you're confident, in control, and ready to engage, making people more likely to approach you.

Consider someone like Barack Obama. His speeches are memorable not just because of what he says but how he says it. He uses expansive, controlled movements, making deliberate gestures that complement his words. His body language radiates confidence and calmness, even in high-stress situations, drawing people in and keeping them engaged.

Creating Presence in a Room

How you **enter a room** says a lot about your confidence. When you walk into a room with purpose, it sets the tone for how others perceive you. There's a difference between slinking in, unnoticed, and walking in with the kind of quiet confidence that commands attention.

One tip is to avoid rushing in. When you walk into a room, take a moment to pause and assess your surroundings. This doesn't mean standing awkwardly at the door, but instead, you move with intention. Walk tall, keep your head up, and make your way into the room calmly and deliberately. It's about occupying space without seeming like you're trying too hard to draw attention. Your body language should signal that you are comfortable in your own skin, and this will automatically make others more drawn to you.

Take, for example, the way a charismatic CEO might enter a meeting. They don't storm into the room or appear overly rushed. Instead, they move with purpose, greet people with a firm handshake and a smile, and make eye contact as they settle in. This creates a sense of authority without being overbearing, and it leaves a lasting impression.

The Subtle Art of Mirroring

One of the most powerful tools for building rapport with others is the **subtle art of mirroring**. This technique involves mimicking the body language, posture, and even tone of voice of the person you're speaking to. Done subtly, it creates a subconscious connection, making the other person feel more comfortable and understood.

Imagine you're at a dinner party and strike up a conversation with someone you've just met. As the conversation progresses, you notice they're leaning slightly forward, so you do the same. They gesture with their hands while speaking, and you begin to mirror those movements, naturally and without exaggeration. By aligning your body language with theirs, you create a sense of synchronicity, making the other person feel like you're on the same wavelength.

Mirroring isn't about mimicking someone like a copycat; it's about creating a rhythm in conversation that feels natural and connected. When done right, it can make you appear more empathetic, attentive, and likable. There are countless examples of suave men using mirroring to build instant rapport. Take the legendary charm of James Bond, for instance. In many of his interactions, Bond doesn't dominate the conversation but rather adapts to the person in front of him, subtly mirroring their body language, which helps him connect with both allies and foes alike. This ability to make others feel understood—without them even realizing why—is one of the hallmarks of persuasive body language.

Recognizing When Others Are Mirroring You

Mirroring can also be a two-way street. Often, when someone feels a strong connection with you, they will begin to mirror your body language unconsciously. This is a powerful signal that rapport has been established. For example, if you're in a negotiation and notice the other person beginning to adopt your posture or gestures, it could be a sign that they're more open to your ideas or that you've successfully built trust.

Recognizing when others are mirroring you gives you valuable insight into how the conversation is progressing. It can help you gauge whether the person is comfortable and engaged or if it might be time to adjust your approach. For instance, if you notice someone leaning in as you speak, it's a good indication that they're interested and invested in what you're saying. On the other hand, if they're pulling back or crossing their arms, it might be a sign that they're becoming disengaged or defensive.

Using Mirroring to Influence

Once you've established rapport, you can use **mirroring** as a way to subtly influence the direction of a conversation. Let's say you're in a business meeting and want to encourage a more relaxed, collaborative atmosphere. By adopting a relaxed posture, lowering your voice slightly, and making open, friendly gestures, you can guide the tone of the conversation in that direction.

Conversely, if you need to project authority or steer the conversation toward more serious topics, you can adjust your body language accordingly. Sitting up straighter, maintaining steady eye contact, and using more deliberate gestures can signal that it's time to focus and get down to business. In many cases, the other person will unconsciously follow your lead, mirroring your body language and aligning with your desired tone.

Conclusion

Projecting confidence and charisma through body language is about more than just standing tall or making eye contact. It's about understanding how to use your body to influence others, build rapport, and create a lasting impression. The power pose, for instance, can change not only how others see you but how you feel about yourself, giving you a boost of confidence before stepping into any high-pressure situation. The way you enter a room, how you use expansive gestures, and even the subtle art of mirroring can help you command attention and form meaningful connections. By mastering these techniques, you'll find that you can navigate any social setting with ease, making yourself the person people naturally gravitate toward—whether in professional or personal scenarios.

In the end, charisma isn't about being the loudest person in the room; it's about understanding the silent signals that make others feel comfortable, connected, and drawn to your presence. When you learn to control and read body language, you gain the ability to speak volumes without saying a word.

Chapter 6: Body Language Mastery – Speaking Volumes Without Saying a Word

Section 3: Using Body Language to Influence and Persuade

Body language speaks louder than words when it comes to persuasion and influence. In many cases, the way you carry yourself, the subtle gestures you use, and how you engage nonverbally can have more impact than anything you might say. Mastering the art of nonverbal communication is a critical tool in influencing others—whether it's to gain trust, negotiate a deal, or simply command attention in a room.

Building Trust Through Nonverbal Cues

Trust is the foundation of influence. People are more likely to be persuaded by someone they feel they can trust. Fortunately, body language plays a significant role in creating that sense of trust, often in ways that words cannot.

For example, open gestures—such as keeping your arms uncrossed and your palms visible—can make you seem approachable and sincere. Think of it like this: when someone is trying to hide something or isn't being completely honest, their body often reveals it. They might cross their arms, avoid showing their hands, or take a step back. These signals suggest defensiveness or even dishonesty. On the other hand, someone who uses open gestures communicates transparency. It's as if they're saying, "I have nothing to hide," which naturally invites trust. I once worked with a colleague who was brilliant but struggled in meetings because of his closed-off body language. His arms were often crossed, he leaned back in his chair, and his brow was perpetually furrowed. Even though his ideas were excellent, people were often hesitant to collaborate with him because he gave off the impression that he wasn't open to feedback or discussion. I suggested he start using more open gestures—sitting forward, uncrossing his arms, and using his hands to emphasize points. Almost immediately, his rapport with others improved, and people began to seek out his input.

Another powerful tool in building trust through body language is **smiling and nodding**. A genuine smile can ease tension, create warmth, and make people feel more comfortable around you. When you nod as someone speaks, it signals that you're actively listening and engaged in what they're saying. But the key here is to be genuine. Overdoing it with too much nodding or forced smiles can come off as insincere. The best approach is to let these gestures come naturally, in response to what's happening in the conversation. For instance, nodding slightly when someone is making a key point shows acknowledgement, whereas a well-timed smile can disarm someone who's feeling tense or uncertain.

Avoiding **closed-off or defensive body language** is essential, especially in high-stakes situations. Crossing your arms, for example, can signal that you're closed off to the conversation, even if you don't intend it that way. The next time you're in a meeting or negotiation, pay attention to how you're standing or sitting. Are your legs or arms crossed? Is your body turned slightly away from the person you're speaking with? These small cues can make a big difference in how others perceive you, and by keeping your posture open, you communicate a willingness to engage and collaborate.

The Power of Silence and Stillness

When we think of influence, we often focus on what we say or how we say it. But sometimes, the most persuasive moments come not from words but from **silence**. Staying still and silent can command attention in a way that speaking cannot. Imagine you're in a heated discussion, and you're the only one who remains calm and composed, while others fidget or speak hurriedly. Your stillness will stand out, signaling that you're in control of your emotions and thoughts.

I recall watching a high-level negotiation between two executives. One of them was eager, almost overly so—talking quickly, gesturing frequently, and making rapid decisions. The other executive, however, maintained a composed stillness, speaking slowly and taking long pauses before responding. While the first executive seemed anxious to get the deal done, the second used silence strategically, creating a sense of anticipation. When he did speak, it carried more weight because he had everyone's full attention. That's the power of

strategic pauses. When you pause, it gives others time to process what you've said, heightening the impact of your words.

In some cases, **silence can be more persuasive than words**, especially in negotiations. When you remain silent after making an offer or a statement, it puts the ball in the other person's court. They feel compelled to fill the silence, and often, they'll reveal more than they intended or make concessions just to break the tension. This is a common tactic in high-stakes negotiations, where the person who can sit comfortably in silence often has the upper hand.

For example, I once witnessed a negotiation where the person trying to close the deal made an offer, then leaned back and said nothing. The other party squirmed in the silence, eventually offering better terms than were originally on the table just to keep the conversation moving. Had the first negotiator jumped in to fill the silence, they might have lost that advantage.

Mastering Eye Contact for Persuasion

Eye contact is one of the most powerful tools of persuasion. When done right, it can convey confidence, sincerity, and attentiveness. But there's a fine line between effective eye contact and making someone uncomfortable. The key is knowing when to maintain it and when to ease off.

In a business setting, for instance, maintaining eye contact while speaking shows that you're confident in your ideas and invested in the conversation. But staring someone down without ever breaking eye contact can come across as aggressive or intimidating. The goal is to strike a balance between **soft and intense eye contact**, depending on the situation. In a more casual conversation, you might soften your gaze and look away occasionally to make the interaction feel more relaxed. But in moments where you need to assert authority or make a persuasive point, maintaining steady, focused eye contact signals conviction.

A good example of this is during presentations. When addressing a group, making eye contact with individuals in the audience creates a sense of connection. It shows that you're engaged with them directly, even though you're speaking to a larger crowd. I remember a mentor of mine giving a speech in front of hundreds of people, yet he had the ability to make it feel like he was speaking to each person individually. He would lock eyes with someone for a few seconds, make his point, and then move on to the next person. This use of eye contact made his speech more persuasive because it felt personal.

One thing to remember is that **eye contact is key to emotional connection** as well. In a social or romantic context, looking someone in the eyes creates a sense of intimacy and trust. It shows that you're fully present and engaged, which makes the other person feel seen and valued. On the flip side, avoiding eye contact can create distance and make people question your sincerity.

However, it's important to be mindful of cultural differences in how eye contact is perceived. In some cultures, maintaining direct eye contact is seen as a sign of confidence and respect, while in others, it can be considered confrontational or disrespectful. Always be aware of these nuances when interacting with people from different backgrounds.

Conclusion

Mastering body language for persuasion is about more than just controlling your gestures or posture. It's about understanding how nonverbal cues like open gestures, stillness, silence, and eye contact can build trust, command attention, and influence others. Whether you're in a business negotiation, a social setting, or simply trying to make a strong impression, the way you use your body speaks volumes.

By cultivating open, approachable body language, you invite trust and connection. By harnessing the power of silence and stillness, you create an air of authority and control. And by mastering the art of eye contact, you can persuade and connect with others on a deeper emotional level. These tools, when used effectively, allow you to influence without overpowering, persuading others with the silent strength of your presence.

Chapter 7: The Suave Man's Guide to Building Authentic Relationships

Section 1: Cultivating Genuine Connections

In a world where fleeting interactions and superficial charm often take center stage, cultivating authentic relationships is a powerful skill that sets a suave man apart. Genuine connections go beyond the surface, building lasting bonds that withstand time and circumstances. Authenticity, more than charm alone, is the true key to unlocking meaningful relationships. Whether in social, professional, or romantic settings, it's the quality of these connections, not the quantity, that truly matters.

The Importance of Authenticity

While charm can open doors, it's authenticity that keeps them open. People can sense when someone is putting on a facade or projecting an image that doesn't align with who they truly are. Superficial charm may dazzle for a moment, but it fades quickly, leaving little behind. On the other hand, authenticity creates a lasting impression, rooted in sincerity.

I remember a friend of mine, Tim, who was incredibly charismatic. He could walk into a room and charm everyone, but those connections rarely lasted. His charm often felt like a performance, a rehearsed act designed to please. Eventually, people began to see through it, realizing that he wasn't being genuine. His relationships faltered because they lacked depth. Tim's experience highlights an important truth: charm alone may attract attention, but it's authenticity that keeps people engaged.

Being authentic means being comfortable with who you are—your strengths, flaws, and everything in between. It means showing vulnerability, which can be a powerful tool in creating deeper connections. When you allow yourself to be vulnerable, you give others permission to do the same, fostering a sense of trust and openness. For example, instead of always trying to present a flawless image, sharing your struggles or uncertainties can make you more relatable. People appreciate honesty, and by being real with them, you create the foundation for a lasting relationship.

One of the most influential leaders I've known was a mentor in my early career. He was a man of few words, but when he spoke, his authenticity was undeniable. He didn't try to impress anyone with big words or grand gestures. Instead, he shared his experiences—both successes and failures—honestly. His vulnerability made people trust him more, and it wasn't long before those around him felt comfortable sharing their own challenges. This openness laid the groundwork for a deep sense of camaraderie that strengthened our team and created an environment where we all felt supported.

Finding Common Ground

Building authentic relationships starts with finding common ground. This isn't about manufacturing connections or forcing shared interests; it's about being genuinely curious about the other person and looking for points of alignment. When you find a shared passion, experience, or value, the conversation flows more naturally, and the connection deepens.

One way to quickly find common ground is by asking open-ended questions that invite the other person to share more about themselves. For instance, instead of asking, "What do you do for a living?" try asking, "What's something you're passionate about in your work?" This subtle shift opens the door for a more meaningful conversation and helps you get to know the person beyond the typical small talk.

Years ago, I attended a networking event where I met a business executive named Marcus. While most people at the event were focused on talking about their companies and titles, Marcus and I found common ground in a shared love for travel. We spent the evening exchanging stories about our adventures around the world, barely touching on work. What started as a casual conversation turned into a strong friendship, and we've stayed in touch ever since. That bond formed not through work, but through our mutual respect for exploration and curiosity about the world.

Finding common ground doesn't always mean discovering a shared hobby or interest. Sometimes it's about aligning values or goals. Perhaps you both value personal growth or are working toward similar professional achievements. When you build relationships based on shared principles, those connections are more likely to endure. In the long run, it's these mutual values that hold relationships together, even when circumstances change.

Mutual respect is the cornerstone of any authentic relationship. Without it, connections remain shallow and transactional. But with respect, even when you and another person have differences, there's a foundation of trust that allows the relationship to grow. This is especially true in professional settings, where differing opinions are common. If both parties approach disagreements with respect, those conversations can actually strengthen the relationship rather than weaken it.

Being a Great Conversationalist

Mastering the art of conversation is central to cultivating genuine relationships. But being a great conversationalist doesn't mean dominating the discussion. Instead, it's about showing a genuine interest in others, asking thoughtful questions, and listening actively. A great conversation is a balance between sharing and listening—between giving and receiving.A few years ago, I met a woman at a social event who had an incredible ability to get people to open up. I watched as she engaged different people in conversation, and one thing stood out: she rarely talked about herself unless asked. Instead, she asked questions that allowed others to share their experiences, ideas, and feelings. She was fully present in every conversation, and people naturally gravitated toward her because they felt heard and understood.

Meaningful questions invite deeper connections. Rather than sticking to surface-level topics, great conversationalists know how to guide the conversation toward more substantial subjects. For example, after some small talk, you might ask, "What's been the most exciting project you've worked on lately?" or "What's something you're looking forward to?" These types of questions open the door for the other person to share something important or personal, which can lead to a more authentic connection.

However, it's important to also share your own experiences and thoughts. A conversation should be a two-way street. When someone opens up to you, reciprocating with your own story or perspective creates balance. But the key is to do so without hijacking the conversation. If someone shares a personal story, respond with empathy and follow-up questions before transitioning to your own experience. This shows that you value what they've said and are genuinely interested in continuing the dialogue.

One of the most underappreciated aspects of conversation is the power of small talk. While many dismiss it as trivial, small talk serves an essential purpose in social interactions. It's a way to break the ice and build rapport before diving into deeper subjects. A light comment about the weather or a compliment on someone's outfit may seem inconsequential, but these brief exchanges create a sense of ease and familiarity. Once that initial connection is made, it becomes easier to transition into more meaningful conversations.

For example, I once met a potential business partner at a conference, and we started our conversation with small talk about the event's food. From there, we naturally shifted to discussing the keynote speaker, which led to a deeper conversation about leadership philosophies. That simple exchange about appetizers laid the groundwork for a relationship that later blossomed into a successful business collaboration.

Conclusion

Authentic relationships are built on a foundation of trust, respect, and genuine interest in others. By embracing authenticity and being willing to show vulnerability, you open the door to deeper, more meaningful connections. Finding common ground—whether through shared interests, goals, or values—helps create bonds that endure over time. And by being a great conversationalist, you show others that you value their experiences and perspectives, which fosters trust and rapport.

Cultivating genuine connections takes time, patience, and effort. It's not about being perfect or always knowing the right thing to say. Instead, it's about being real, present, and truly invested in the relationships you build. As a suave man, these authentic relationships will become your greatest asset, both personally and professionally.

Chapter 7: The Suave Man's Guide to Building Authentic Relationships

Section 2: The Art of Networking Like a Suave Man

In the world of networking, where the noise of self-promotion often drowns out genuine interaction, the suave man stands apart. Networking isn't just about collecting business cards or adding LinkedIn connections; it's about building and nurturing authentic relationships that provide mutual value. This approach not only enhances your personal and professional life but also cultivates a network of people who genuinely value and support you.

Building a Strong Personal Network

To network effectively, it's crucial to approach it as an opportunity for relationship-building rather than mere self-promotion. Think of networking as planting seeds that, with time and care, will grow into fruitful relationships. It's less about talking up your achievements and more about understanding and supporting others.

A good friend of mine, Alan, embodies this approach. Alan is a successful entrepreneur who rarely talks about his accomplishments when networking. Instead, he focuses on learning about the people he meets, asking them about their goals and challenges. Alan's genuine curiosity and interest in others make him a sought-after connection. By prioritizing relationship-building over self-promotion, Alan has created a network of people who genuinely appreciate his support and are eager to return the favor.

Maintaining relationships over time doesn't require constant, intensive effort. Simple gestures can keep connections fresh. For instance, sending a quick message to check in, sharing an interesting article relevant to someone's field, or remembering important milestones like birthdays or anniversaries can go a long way. These small acts of consideration remind people that you value them and their relationship, without feeling like a chore.

I remember when I moved to a new city and needed to establish a network from scratch. Instead of focusing solely on my own needs, I made it a point to stay in touch with the people I met. I would drop a note about a book they might find interesting or invite them to casual gatherings. These small efforts helped me build a solid network where relationships were reciprocal and supportive.

Leveraging your network should always be done with mutual benefit in mind. Avoid the temptation to appear opportunistic by ensuring that any request or favor is accompanied by something of value for the other person. For example, if you're seeking advice or a referral, consider what you can offer in return. This could be sharing your own expertise, making a valuable introduction, or offering to help with a project. When both parties benefit, relationships strengthen and trust builds.

Navigating High-Stakes Social Events

High-stakes social events, whether professional conferences or upscale social gatherings, present unique challenges. To make an impact without being overbearing, start by focusing on quality over quantity. It's more effective to have a few meaningful conversations than to attempt superficial interactions with everyone in the room.

At a recent industry conference, I found myself in a room filled with high-profile professionals. Instead of trying to meet everyone, I concentrated on engaging deeply with a few key individuals. I approached each conversation with genuine curiosity and listened actively, which allowed me to connect on a more meaningful level. By showing that I valued their insights and experiences, I made a lasting impression and built connections that were more substantial than the typical networking interactions.

When working a room, your presence is key. This doesn't mean dominating the conversation but rather being memorable in a positive way. Approach people with confidence, maintain open body language, and be genuinely interested in their responses. A warm smile and a firm handshake can set the tone for a positive interaction. It's also essential to read the room and adjust your approach based on the energy and dynamics you observe.

Following up after events is crucial to solidifying connections. A thoughtful follow-up message, referencing a specific point from your conversation, shows that you were genuinely engaged and appreciated the interaction. For instance, if someone mentioned a recent project they were excited about, you could send a note expressing your interest and asking how it's going. This kind of follow-up not only reinforces the connection but also demonstrates that you value their input and are committed to maintaining the relationship.

Becoming a Connector

Being a connector means taking an active role in facilitating relationships between people in your network. This doesn't just benefit others; it also enhances your own influence and status. When you introduce people who could benefit from knowing each other, you position yourself as a valuable resource and a facilitator of meaningful connections.

One of the most impactful ways to become a connector is by identifying opportunities where people in your network could benefit from each other's expertise. For example, if you know someone looking for a new job in a specific industry and another person who is hiring in that field, making an introduction can be incredibly valuable. This kind of proactive connection not only helps the individuals involved but also strengthens your reputation as someone who adds value.

A mentor of mine, Richard, is a master connector. He has a knack for remembering people's needs and goals and making thoughtful introductions. When Richard introduced me to a potential business partner, it wasn't just a random connection; he had taken the time to understand both our interests and how we could complement each other. This introduction led to a fruitful partnership and reinforced Richard's reputation as someone who genuinely supports others.

The act of connecting people also helps you build stronger relationships with those you introduce. When you facilitate meaningful connections, people remember you as someone who contributed to their success. This fosters goodwill and a sense of reciprocity, where others are more likely to support you in return.

Conclusion

Networking like a suave man isn't about flashy tactics or superficial charm. It's about building authentic relationships through genuine interest, thoughtful follow-ups, and proactive connecting. By approaching networking as a means of relationship-building rather than self-promotion, you create a network that is supportive, reciprocal, and enduring.

Navigating high-stakes events with grace and making a memorable impact involves focusing on quality interactions and following up thoughtfully. Becoming a connector adds value not just to those you introduce but also to your own network, enhancing your influence and reputation.

In the world of networking, where many are focused on what they can get, the suave man stands out by emphasizing what he can give. This approach doesn't just build a network of contacts; it fosters a community of genuine relationships that offer mutual support and lasting value.

Chapter 7: The Suave Man's Guide to Building Authentic Relationships

Section 3: Building Relationships with Emotional Depth

Building relationships with emotional depth is the hallmark of a truly suave individual. It's not just about surface-level charm or making an impression; it's about forging connections that are meaningful and enduring. This level of emotional engagement requires empathy, understanding, and a genuine investment in the well-being of others. In this section, we'll explore how to cultivate relationships that resonate on a deeper level, from demonstrating empathy to balancing charm and depth in romantic relationships, and sustaining long-term friendships.

Showing Empathy and Understanding

Empathy is the cornerstone of authentic relationships. It's about more than just listening; it's about truly understanding and connecting with the emotions of others. One of my close friends, Jenna, exemplifies this quality in her interactions. When someone is speaking to her, she doesn't just nod along; she actively engages by acknowledging their feelings and providing thoughtful feedback.

For example, when her colleague faced a challenging work situation, Jenna didn't just offer generic advice. Instead, she listened intently, reflected back what she heard, and validated her colleague's feelings without jumping to solutions or offering unsolicited opinions. "It sounds like you're really stressed about this project, and I can understand why," Jenna said. "It's a tough situation. How can I support you in this?"

This approach builds trust and loyalty because it shows that you genuinely care about the other person's experience. Validation doesn't mean you have to agree or disagree; it's about acknowledging the other person's perspective and emotions. By showing empathy, you create a safe space for open and honest communication, which strengthens the relationship and fosters a deeper connection.

Balancing Charm and Depth in Romantic Relationships

Romantic relationships thrive on emotional intimacy and vulnerability. While charm can initially attract someone, it's the emotional depth that sustains a romantic bond. I remember a couple, Mark and Lisa, who started their relationship with undeniable chemistry. Mark was charismatic and had a knack for making Lisa laugh, but it was his willingness to be vulnerable and share his true self that deepened their connection.

During one of their early dates, Mark opened up about his struggles with self-doubt and how it affected his life. Instead of keeping up a facade of constant confidence, he shared his insecurities and fears. This level of vulnerability allowed Lisa to see him as a real person, not just someone who was charming and funny. It created a space for Lisa to also share her own experiences, and they both began to connect on a more profound level.

Charm in romantic relationships is important, but it's the emotional intimacy that builds a lasting bond. To achieve this, you need to be willing to share your authentic self, including your fears, dreams, and vulnerabilities. Encourage your partner to do the same by showing genuine interest in their emotions and experiences. This balance of charm and depth helps cultivate a relationship that's not only enjoyable but also deeply fulfilling.

Sustaining Long-Term Friendships

Maintaining lasting friendships requires consistent effort, mutual support, and a willingness to grow together. True friends are those who support you through life's ups and downs, and sustaining these relationships means being there for each other over the long haul. I have a friend, Sam, with whom I've shared a friendship for over a decade. Our bond has endured because of the way we support each other through various life stages.

Sam and I have weathered many changes—career shifts, moves, and personal challenges. What has kept our friendship strong is our mutual commitment to supporting one another and growing together. We make an effort to stay in touch regularly, even if it's just a quick call or a message. We celebrate each other's achievements and offer support during tough times. This consistent effort helps keep the friendship vibrant and meaningful.

At the same time, giving each other space is just as important as spending time together. True friendship doesn't demand constant attention or proximity. There are times when both of us have been caught up in work or personal matters, but our friendship remains strong because we respect each other's need for space and independence. Understanding that friendships can ebb and flow, and accepting that periods of distance are normal, helps maintain a healthy and enduring connection.

Handling conflicts in friendships requires tact and understanding. Disagreements are natural, but addressing them with empathy and a willingness to understand the other person's perspective is crucial. For example, when Sam and I had a falling out over a miscommunication, we took the time to discuss our feelings openly. Instead of letting the issue fester, we approached it with a mindset of resolving the misunderstanding and strengthening our bond. This approach not only resolved the conflict but also reinforced our commitment to each other.

Conclusion

Building relationships with emotional depth involves more than just superficial interactions. It requires a genuine investment in understanding and connecting with others on an emotional level. Showing empathy, balancing charm with vulnerability in romantic relationships, and sustaining long-term friendships all contribute to creating bonds that are meaningful and enduring.

By demonstrating empathy and understanding, you build trust and loyalty. Balancing charm with emotional depth in romantic relationships fosters a connection that goes beyond surface attraction. Sustaining long-term friendships involves mutual support, respect for personal space, and effective conflict resolution. These principles guide the suave man in creating and nurturing relationships that are not only charming but also profoundly rewarding.

Incorporating these strategies into your relationships can transform them from casual interactions into deep, meaningful connections that enrich your life and the lives of those around you.

Chapter 8: The Suave Man's Path to Lifelong Personal Growth

Section 1: Committing to Continuous Improvement

Personal growth is an ongoing journey rather than a destination. For the suave man, embracing continuous improvement is not just about refining charm and confidence but also about developing a deeper understanding of oneself and others. This journey involves self-reflection, setting and achieving goals, and cultivating a growth mindset. In this section, we'll explore how these elements can drive lifelong personal growth.

The Power of Self-Reflection

Self-reflection is a powerful tool for personal growth. It allows you to pause, look inward, and evaluate your experiences and behaviors. I remember a time when a colleague of mine, Alex, decided to take a more introspective approach to his personal development. After a challenging year at work, Alex felt that something was missing in his approach to leadership and communication.

He began keeping a journal, not just about his daily activities but about his reactions, feelings, and interactions with others. Over time, he noticed patterns in his behavior that he hadn't been aware of before. For instance, he realized that he often interrupted others during meetings, not out of disregard but out of excitement to contribute. Recognizing this pattern allowed Alex to work on his listening skills, making him a more effective and empathetic leader.

Journaling and introspection are more than just self-indulgent practices; they are crucial for understanding your strengths and weaknesses. By regularly assessing your actions and reactions, you gain insight into areas where you excel and areas that need improvement. This self-awareness fosters a deeper understanding of your motivations and helps you to be more intentional about your personal growth.

Being open to change and new perspectives is another vital aspect of self-reflection. As you gain insight into your behavior, you may encounter aspects of yourself that are uncomfortable to confront. Embracing these revelations, rather than avoiding them, is essential for growth. For instance, if you discover that you tend to react defensively to criticism, acknowledging this trait allows you to address it and develop a more constructive response to feedback.

Setting Personal and Social Goals

Setting goals is a practical way to channel your desire for improvement into tangible outcomes. However, it's important that these goals are both challenging and attainable. For example, when I first started focusing on enhancing my social skills, I set a goal to attend at least one networking event per month. This goal was challenging enough to push me out of my comfort zone but attainable within my schedule.

Tracking your progress is crucial for maintaining motivation and measuring your growth. I found it helpful to keep a record of each event I attended and note my observations and outcomes. This practice allowed me to see incremental improvements and identify areas where I needed to focus more attention. Celebrating small wins along the way, such as successfully starting a conversation with a stranger or receiving positive feedback, kept me motivated and reinforced my commitment to growth.

Setting personal and social goals also involves reflecting on what you want to achieve in different areas of your life. Whether it's improving your charm, building better relationships, or advancing your career, having clear goals helps you stay focused and aligned with your aspirations. For instance, if your goal is to become a more charismatic conversationalist, you might set specific objectives such as learning new techniques for engaging others or practicing active listening in conversations.

Embracing a Growth Mindset

A growth mindset is the belief that your abilities and intelligence can be developed through dedication and hard work. This perspective is crucial for personal growth as it encourages you to view challenges as opportunities for improvement rather than obstacles.

One of the most impactful lessons I learned about embracing a growth mindset came from a friend, Sara, who was an accomplished public speaker. Early in her career, Sara faced a particularly challenging speaking engagement where she struggled with a technical issue during her presentation. Instead of viewing this experience as a failure, Sara saw it as a chance to learn and improve.

She analyzed the situation, identified what went wrong, and sought feedback from peers. This constructive approach not only helped her to enhance her skills but also reinforced her resilience and adaptability. Sara's experience illustrates how a growth mindset can turn setbacks into valuable learning experiences.

Staying curious and eager to learn is another key aspect of a growth mindset. By remaining open to new ideas and experiences, you continuously expand your knowledge and skills. Surrounding yourself with people who push you to grow can also be incredibly beneficial. These individuals challenge you, provide valuable feedback, and inspire you to reach new heights. For example, my mentor, Tom, always encouraged me to step out of my comfort zone and take on new challenges. His belief in my potential pushed me to strive for excellence and embrace growth opportunities.

Incorporating a growth mindset into your daily life means actively seeking out opportunities to learn and improve. Whether it's through reading books, attending workshops, or engaging in meaningful conversations, staying curious and open to new experiences fosters continuous personal development.

Conclusion

The path to lifelong personal growth involves a commitment to self-reflection, goal-setting, and embracing a growth mindset. By regularly assessing your strengths and weaknesses, setting attainable goals, and remaining open to change, you pave the way for continuous improvement. A growth mindset transforms challenges into opportunities and fosters a lifelong eagerness to learn and develop.

As you embark on this journey, remember that personal growth is not a destination but a lifelong process. Embrace the challenges, celebrate the victories, and remain dedicated to becoming the best version of yourself. By doing so, you not only enhance your charm and confidence but also enrich your life and the lives of those around you.

Chapter 8: The Suave Man's Path to Lifelong Personal Growth

Section 1: Committing to Continuous Improvement

Personal growth is an ongoing journey rather than a destination. For the suave man, embracing continuous improvement is not just about refining charm and confidence but also about developing a deeper understanding of oneself and others. This journey involves self-reflection, setting and achieving goals, and cultivating a growth mindset. In this section, we'll explore how these elements can drive lifelong personal growth.

The Power of Self-Reflection

Self-reflection is a powerful tool for personal growth. It allows you to pause, look inward, and evaluate your experiences and behaviors. I remember a time when a colleague of mine, Alex, decided to take a more introspective approach to his personal development. After a challenging year at work, Alex felt that something was missing in his approach to leadership and communication.

He began keeping a journal, not just about his daily activities but about his reactions, feelings, and interactions with others. Over time, he noticed patterns in his behavior that he hadn't been aware of before. For instance, he realized that he often interrupted others during meetings, not out of disregard but out of excitement to contribute. Recognizing this pattern allowed Alex to work on his listening skills, making him a more effective and empathetic leader.

Journaling and introspection are more than just self-indulgent practices; they are crucial for understanding your strengths and weaknesses. By regularly assessing your actions and reactions, you gain insight into areas where you excel and areas that need improvement. This self-awareness fosters a deeper understanding of your motivations and helps you to be more intentional about your personal growth.

Being open to change and new perspectives is another vital aspect of self-reflection. As you gain insight into your behavior, you may encounter aspects of yourself that are uncomfortable to confront. Embracing these revelations, rather than avoiding them, is essential for growth. For instance, if you discover that you tend to react defensively to criticism, acknowledging this trait allows you to address it and develop a more constructive response to feedback.

Setting Personal and Social Goals

Setting goals is a practical way to channel your desire for improvement into tangible outcomes. However, it's important that these goals are both challenging and attainable. For example, when I first started focusing on enhancing my social skills, I set a goal to attend at least one networking event per month. This goal was challenging enough to push me out of my comfort zone but attainable within my schedule.

Tracking your progress is crucial for maintaining motivation and measuring your growth. I found it helpful to keep a record of each event I attended and note my observations and outcomes. This practice allowed me to see incremental improvements and identify areas where I needed to focus more attention. Celebrating small wins along the way, such as successfully starting a conversation with a stranger or receiving positive feedback, kept me motivated and reinforced my commitment to growth.

Setting personal and social goals also involves reflecting on what you want to achieve in different areas of your life. Whether it's improving your charm, building better relationships, or advancing your career, having clear goals helps you stay focused and aligned with your aspirations. For instance, if your goal is to become a more charismatic conversationalist, you might set specific objectives such as learning new techniques for engaging others or practicing active listening in conversations.

Embracing a Growth Mindset

A growth mindset is the belief that your abilities and intelligence can be developed through dedication and hard work. This perspective is crucial for personal growth as it encourages you to view challenges as opportunities for improvement rather than obstacles. One of the most impactful lessons I learned about embracing a growth mindset came from a friend, Sara, who was an accomplished public speaker. Early in her career, Sara faced a particularly challenging speaking engagement where she struggled with a technical issue during her presentation. Instead of viewing this experience as a failure, Sara saw it as a chance to learn and improve.

She analyzed the situation, identified what went wrong, and sought feedback from peers. This constructive approach not only helped her to enhance her skills but also reinforced her resilience and adaptability. Sara's experience illustrates how a growth mindset can turn setbacks into valuable learning experiences.

Staying curious and eager to learn is another key aspect of a growth mindset. By remaining open to new ideas and experiences, you continuously expand your knowledge and skills. Surrounding yourself with people who push you to grow can also be incredibly beneficial. These individuals challenge you, provide valuable feedback, and inspire you to reach new heights. For example, my mentor, Tom, always encouraged me to step out of my comfort zone and take on new challenges. His belief in my potential pushed me to strive for excellence and embrace growth opportunities.

Incorporating a growth mindset into your daily life means actively seeking out opportunities to learn and improve. Whether it's through reading books, attending workshops, or engaging in meaningful conversations, staying curious and open to new experiences fosters continuous personal development.

Conclusion

The path to lifelong personal growth involves a commitment to self-reflection, goal-setting, and embracing a growth mindset. By regularly assessing your strengths and weaknesses, setting attainable goals, and remaining open to change, you pave the way for continuous improvement. A growth mindset transforms challenges into opportunities and fosters a lifelong eagerness to learn and develop.

As you embark on this journey, remember that personal growth is not a destination but a lifelong process. Embrace the challenges, celebrate the victories, and remain dedicated to becoming the best version of yourself. By doing so, you not only enhance your charm and confidence but also enrich your life and the lives of those around you.

Chapter 8: The Suave Man's Path to Lifelong Personal Growth

Section 2: Expanding Your Comfort Zone

Expanding your comfort zone is more than just a personal challenge; it's a transformative journey that enhances your social charm, boosts confidence, and opens doors to new opportunities. The path to growth often involves stepping into unfamiliar territory, embracing discomfort, and learning from experiences that push your boundaries. In this section, we'll explore practical ways to expand your comfort zone, drawing from personal experiences and stories to illustrate the benefits of embracing new challenges.

Taking Risks in Social Situations

Stepping out of your comfort zone in social situations can be daunting, but it is essential for personal growth. I recall a pivotal moment early in my career when I was invited to a high-profile networking event. The attendees were influential figures in my industry, and the idea of mingling with them was intimidating.

I could have easily avoided the event, but instead, I decided to embrace the discomfort.

At the event, I made a conscious effort to engage with people I didn't know, initiating conversations and asking thoughtful questions. While it was challenging at first, the experience taught me valuable lessons about confidence and social skills. I learned that discomfort often precedes growth, and by pushing through it, I not only improved my networking abilities but also expanded my professional circle.

Taking risks in social situations means challenging yourself to engage in activities that make you uncomfortable but ultimately lead to personal and social development. Whether it's starting a conversation with a stranger, attending an unfamiliar social gathering, or taking on a leadership role in a group, these experiences push you to grow. The more you expose yourself to these situations, the more comfortable and confident you become.

One practical challenge to consider is setting a goal to attend one new social event or networking opportunity each month. By regularly placing yourself in new environments, you gradually build the skills and confidence needed to handle a variety of social situations with ease.

Cultivating Diverse Experiences

Cultivating diverse experiences is another effective way to expand your comfort zone and enhance your personal growth. Traveling to new places and immersing yourself in different cultures provides invaluable insights and broadens your perspective. I remember a trip I took to Southeast Asia, where I spent several weeks exploring local customs, languages, and cuisines. The experience was eye-opening and deeply enriching.

Traveling forces you to adapt to new environments and navigate unfamiliar situations, which fosters resilience and adaptability. It also exposes you to diverse perspectives and ways of life, enriching your understanding of the world and enhancing your social charm. Engaging with people from different backgrounds helps you become more empathetic and culturally aware, qualities that are highly valued in social interactions.

In addition to traveling, taking up new hobbies and learning new skills contribute to becoming more well-rounded. For instance, when I decided to learn a new language, it not only improved my cognitive abilities but also opened up opportunities for meaningful connections with people from different cultures. Each new skill or hobby you pursue adds depth to your character and provides additional talking points in social situations.

Surrounding yourself with diverse perspectives is equally important for personal growth. Engaging with people who have different backgrounds, experiences, and viewpoints challenges your assumptions and broadens your understanding. This exposure helps you develop a more nuanced perspective on various issues and enhances your ability to connect with others on a deeper level.

Learning from Failure and Rejection

Learning from failure and rejection is a crucial aspect of expanding your comfort zone. Failure is often perceived as a setback, but it can be a powerful learning tool. I experienced this firsthand when I failed to secure a major client early in my career. Instead of viewing failure as a reflection of my abilities, I chose to see it as an opportunity for growth.

I took time to analyze what went wrong, sought feedback, and identified areas for improvement. This reflective approach allowed me to refine my skills and strategies, ultimately leading to greater success in future endeavors. By reframing failure as a learning experience, you build resilience and gain valuable insights that contribute to your long-term growth.

Developing resilience in the face of social rejection or missteps is essential for maintaining confidence and motivation. When faced with rejection, it's easy to become discouraged, but it's important to remember that rejection is a natural part of the growth process. Each rejection provides an opportunity to learn, adapt, and improve. For example, if a social interaction doesn't go as planned, use it as a chance to reflect on what you could do differently next time.

Every setback is a stepping stone to greater success. Embracing this mindset helps you stay focused on your goals and persevere through challenges. The more you practice this approach, the more resilient you become, and the better equipped you are to handle future obstacles.

Conclusion

Expanding your comfort zone is a transformative process that involves taking risks, cultivating diverse experiences, and learning from failure. By actively seeking opportunities to step outside of your comfort zone, you build confidence, enhance your social charm, and open yourself up to new possibilities.

The stories of personal growth and success illustrate that embracing discomfort and challenges is key to unlocking your full potential. Whether it's engaging in new social situations, exploring different cultures, or learning from setbacks, each experience contributes to your development as a more well-rounded and confident individual.

As you continue on your path to lifelong personal growth, remember that the journey of expanding your comfort zone is ongoing. Embrace the challenges, celebrate your progress, and remain committed to pushing your boundaries. By doing so, you not only enhance your own life but also enrich the lives of those around you.

Chapter 8: The Suave Man's Path to Lifelong Personal Growth

Section 3: Staying Suave for Life

The journey to becoming a suave individual doesn't end with mastering charm, confidence, and social finesse. True suavity is about maintaining these qualities throughout your life and evolving them as you age. Staying suave for life means adapting to the changes that come with time, leaving a lasting impact on those around you, and continuously committing to personal growth. Let's explore how to stay suave as you grow older, build a lasting legacy, and commit to lifelong learning.

Maintaining Your Charm as You Grow Older

Charm, confidence, and finesse are not just youthful traits; they are timeless qualities that can evolve and mature as you age. When I think about the enduring charm of some of the most charismatic individuals I've encountered, I am struck by their ability to adapt and refine their charm over time. Take, for instance, my mentor, Richard, a man in his seventies who still captivates people with his charisma. What makes Richard stand out is not just his charming demeanor but his ability to adapt his style and presence to suit his age and experience.

As you grow older, maintaining your charm involves evolving your style while staying relevant. It's about transitioning from the energetic charm of youth to a more refined and sophisticated presence. Richard's approach is a testament to this. He has embraced a more classic and elegant style of dress and refined his conversational skills to reflect his wealth of experience. This evolution doesn't mean abandoning what makes you charming; rather, it's about enhancing it to align with your current stage in life.

Avoiding complacency is crucial. Complacency can erode the charm and confidence you've worked so hard to build. To stay sharp socially and mentally, engage in activities that challenge you. Continue pursuing interests and hobbies that stimulate your mind and keep you engaged with the world around you. Richard, for instance, keeps up with current affairs, reads widely, and actively participates in community events. His commitment to staying informed and involved helps him maintain his charm and relevance in conversations.

The Suave Man's Legacy

Leaving a lasting impact involves more than just being charming; it's about building a reputation as a person of substance. Richard's legacy is not just in his charm but in the way he has mentored and influenced others. When you think of creating a legacy, consider how you can positively impact those around you.

Mentorship is a powerful way to leave a lasting mark. By sharing your experiences, insights, and the principles of charm and confidence with the next generation, you contribute to their growth and success. Richard has mentored numerous young professionals, offering guidance and support as they navigate their careers. His influence extends beyond his personal charm, shaping the lives of those he has helped.

Building a reputation as a man of substance involves demonstrating integrity, wisdom, and reliability. Charm alone isn't enough; it's the combination of charm with these deeper qualities that makes a lasting impact. By living authentically and consistently, you earn the respect and admiration of others, solidifying your legacy.

Passing on the principles of charm and confidence is not just about teaching techniques but about embodying these qualities in your interactions. Share the principles you've learned through your experiences and show how they can be applied in different contexts. Your actions and the way you handle various situations serve as a living example for others to follow.

Committing to Lifelong Learning

A commitment to lifelong learning is essential for staying suave throughout your life. The world is constantly evolving, and to remain relevant, you must stay curious and open to new ideas. My friend Alex, a successful entrepreneur, exemplifies this commitment. Despite his achievements, he remains a lifelong learner, continuously seeking to expand his knowledge and refine his skills.

Staying curious and eager to learn is not just about formal education but about being open to new experiences and perspectives. Engage in activities that challenge your thinking and broaden your horizons. Attend workshops, read books, and explore new areas of interest. Lifelong learning helps you adapt to changes, stay mentally sharp, and maintain your social charm.

Adaptability is crucial in a changing world. As social norms, technologies, and cultural contexts shift, being adaptable ensures that you remain effective and relevant. Embrace change as an opportunity for growth rather than a threat. By staying adaptable, you can navigate new situations with ease and continue to engage with others in a meaningful way.

Humility is another important aspect of lifelong learning. Recognize that there is always more to learn and room for improvement. Even as you accumulate knowledge and experience, remain open to feedback and new ideas. Humility helps you stay grounded and receptive to learning opportunities, which in turn enhances your charm and social skills.

Conclusion

Staying suave for life is about more than just maintaining your charm; it's about evolving with grace, leaving a meaningful impact, and committing to ongoing personal growth. By adapting your style and presence as you age, building a legacy through mentorship and substance, and embracing lifelong learning, you ensure that your suave qualities endure and continue to enrich your life and the lives of those around you.

The journey to lifelong personal growth and suavity is continuous. It involves staying curious, adapting to change, and nurturing your relationships with authenticity and depth. Embrace these principles with dedication and enthusiasm, and you'll not only maintain your charm but also inspire others to embark on their own path to lifelong growth.

Book Description

"The Recipe of a Suave, Charming Man: Mastering Confidence, Charm, and Finesse"

Unlock the secrets to unparalleled charisma and lasting success with "The Suave Man's Guide: Mastering Charm, Confidence, and Lifelong Personal Growth." This comprehensive eBook is your ultimate roadmap to becoming magnetic in every social and professional setting.

In this guide, you'll explore the foundational elements of charm and confidence, learning how to harness them to captivate and influence those around you. From mastering first impressions to navigating complex social dynamics, you'll gain insights into effective communication, body language, and the art of persuasion. Discover how to adapt your approach across various situations, build authentic relationships, and handle conflicts with finesse.

Delve into the science of emotional intelligence and understand how to read and respond to social cues, creating connections that resonate on a deeper level. Learn how to maintain your charm as you age, leaving a legacy of influence and mentorship that endures over time.With practical advice and real-life stories, this eBook provides actionable strategies for expanding your comfort zone, embracing continuous growth, and staying suave throughout your life. Whether you're seeking to enhance your social skills, build meaningful relationships, or achieve personal and professional success, "The Suave Man's Guide" is your essential companion on the path to becoming the best version of yourself

Embrace the power of charm and confidence and embark on a journey of lifelong personal development. Your transformation starts here.

Hello my name is Anthony Wilson, 40yrs and the author of this manuscript of charm and suave insight. My quest is to help as many men as I can with the knowledge and experience I have collected throughout my life. I believe it would help guide men 18-60 to greatness in their personal and professional lives. I've gone through many phases in my life and they have all led me back to the game. The game of life, the development of oneself in such a way that he can not be denied in the life that he makes for himself. Take heed to all the information in this manuscript for this might be the step you need or another tool to add onto the skills that you have already obtained. Become the person that takes action, that knows what they want and knows how to get the resources to do so. Become the person that your family admirers, also the one they turn to in order to solve a problem because you have the knowledge and game to get the job done. I set out on my journey in order to break generational curses and in turn create generational wealth for my family and myself. Focus on yourself with the intent to evolve every aspect of your life, for this is a strategy guide that details ways on which to win in life. generational wealth for my family and myself. Focus on yourself with the intent to evolve every aspect of your life, for this is a strategy guide that details ways on which to win in life.

"Some things can't be learned they must be remembered"

ACKNOWLEDGEMENT

Dear Reader,

Thank you. Not just for turning these pages, but for opening your mind to the vast potential that lies within you. You've allowed me to share not just a perspective, but a blueprint for a life imbued with greater depth, connection, and understanding. In an age where distractions are constant and superficiality often reigns, you've chosen to seek something more. That choice alone sets you apart.

Think of this journey like a voyage through the cosmos. Every interaction, every relationship, is a star in the vast constellation of your life. And just as the universe is governed by laws that reveal the beauty and order in what might first appear chaotic, so too are there principles that can bring harmony to our human connections. You've been willing to explore these principles, to question, and to grow. That's the first step toward transformation.

The insights and techniques we've explored together aren't mere tricks or tactics. They are tools for elevating your life, for seeing the world not just as it is, but as it could be. Like a telescope revealing the hidden wonders of the night sky, this knowledge can help you perceive the extraordinary potential in everyday moments and the people around you.

By embracing these ideas, you are not only enriching your own existence but also the lives of those you touch. You become a catalyst for positive change, a beacon that others can look to. And in this interconnected journey, we find that personal growth isn't just about self-improvement; it's about creating a ripple effect that transforms the world around us.

So, thank you for your curiosity, your willingness to venture beyond the familiar, and your commitment to becoming the best version of yourself. The universe favors the bold, and you, my friend, are now equipped to explore its boundless possibilities.

With gratitude and admiration,

[Anthony B Wilson]

About the Author

Hello my name is Anthony Wilson, 40yrs and the author of this manuscript of charm and suave insight. My quest is to help as many men as I can with the knowledge and experience I have collected throughout my life. I believe it would help guide men 18-60 to greatness in their personal and professional lives. I've gone through many phases in my life and they have all led me back to the game. The game of life, the development of oneself in such a way that he can not be denied in the life that he makes for himself. Take heed to all the information in this manuscript for this might be the step you need or another tool to add onto the skills that you have already obtained. Become the person that takes action, that knows what they want and knows how to get the resources to do so. Become the person that your family admirers, also the one they turn to in order to solve a problem because you have the knowledge and game to get the job done. I set out on my journey in order to break generational curses and in turn create generational wealth for my family and myself. Focus on yourself with the intent to evolve every aspect of your life, for this is a strategy guide that details ways on which to win in life. generational wealth for my family and myself. Focus on yourself with the intent to evolve every aspect of your life, for this is a strategy guide that details ways on which to win in life.

"Some things can't be learned they must be remembered"
Read more at wilsonab826@gmail.com.